DOG GROOMING ENCYCLOPEDIA

A Complete Guide to Professional and At-Home Coat Care, Bathing, Trimming, Nail Care, Teeth Care, Ear Care and Overall Maintenance for All Breeds and Coat Types

DR. RUBY LUCAS

Copyright © 2024 by Dr. Ruby Lucas

All rights reserved. No part of this book may be reproduced, distributed, or transmitted in any form or by any means, including photocopying, recording, or other electronic or mechanical methods, without the prior written permission of the author, except in the case of brief quotations embodied in reviews and certain other non-commercial uses permitted by copyright law.

Table of Content

INTRODUCTION — 8

- GROOMING AND PHYSICAL HEALTH — 8
- EMOTIONAL AND BEHAVIORAL BENEFITS OF GROOMING — 9
- PREVENTIVE CARE THROUGH GROOMING — 10
- GROOMING AS A FOUNDATION FOR LIFELONG HEALTH — 11
- BEYOND THE BASICS: GROOMING AS A LIFESTYLE — 12

CHAPTER 1: UNDERSTANDING DOG GROOMING BASICS — 13

- THE ANATOMY OF A DOG'S COAT — 14
- DIFFERENT COAT TYPES AND THEIR GROOMING NEEDS — 19
- TOOLS OF THE TRADE: BRUSHES, CLIPPERS, SCISSORS, AND MORE — 25
  - BRUSHES: ESSENTIAL FOR MAINTENANCE AND HEALTH — 25
  - CLIPPERS: KEEPING THE COAT TRIMMED AND TIDY — 27
  - SCISSORS: PRECISION GROOMING FOR A FLAWLESS LOOK — 28
  - COMBS: DETANGLING AND FINISHING TOUCHES — 29
  - OTHER TOOLS FOR A COMPLETE GROOMING KIT — 30
- GROOMING SAFETY AND PRECAUTIONS — 31
  - HANDLING YOUR DOG DURING GROOMING — 32
  - USING THE RIGHT TOOLS SAFELY — 33
  - GROOMING SENSITIVE AREAS SAFELY — 35
  - RECOGNIZING SIGNS OF STRESS OR DISCOMFORT — 36

CHAPTER 2: BATHING AND HYGIENE — 38

- WHEN AND HOW TO BATHE YOUR DOG — 39
  - WHEN TO BATHE YOUR DOG — 39
  - HOW TO BATHE YOUR DOG — 41
- SELECTING THE RIGHT SHAMPOOS AND CONDITIONERS — 44
  - KEY INGREDIENTS TO LOOK FOR IN DOG SHAMPOOS AND CONDITIONERS — 47
  - TYPES OF DOG SHAMPOOS AND CONDITIONERS — 49

CLEANING EARS, EYES, AND TEETH	51
Cleaning Your Dog's Ears	51
Cleaning Your Dog's Eyes	53
Cleaning Your Dog's Teeth	55
MANAGING SHEDDING AND DANDER	**57**
Managing Shedding Through Grooming	59
Managing Dander in Dogs	60

CHAPTER 3: COAT CARE TECHNIQUES   63

Brushing for Different Coat Types	64
TRIMMING AND STYLING ESSENTIALS	**69**
DEALING WITH MATS, TANGLES, AND KNOTS	**76**
Causes of Mats and Tangles	76
Preventing Mats, Tangles, and Knots	78
How to Remove Mats, Tangles, and Knots	79
Working with Sensitive Areas	81
When to Seek Professional Help	81
SEASONAL GROOMING TIPS	**82**
Spring Grooming Tips	82
Summer Grooming Tips	84
Fall Grooming Tips	86
Winter Grooming Tips	87

CHAPTER 4: NAIL, PAW, AND SKIN CARE   89

NAIL TRIMMING: TOOLS AND TECHNIQUES	**90**
Tools for Nail Trimming	91
Proper Techniques for Nail Trimming	93
Paw Pad Care and Moisturizing	95
Techniques for Moisturizing Your Dog's Paw Pads	100
IDENTIFYING AND TREATING SKIN CONDITIONS IN DOGS	**102**
Common Dog Skin Conditions	103

CHAPTER 5: SPECIALIZED GROOMING   111

GROOMING PUPPIES: A GENTLE START	112
GROOMING OLDER DOGS AND DOGS WITH SPECIAL NEEDS	117
UNDERSTANDING THE NEEDS OF OLDER DOGS	117
GROOMING FOR DOGS WITH MEDICAL CONDITIONS	124
THE IMPORTANCE OF GROOMING FOR DOGS WITH MEDICAL CONDITIONS	124
GROOMING DOGS WITH SKIN CONDITIONS	125
GROOMING DOGS WITH MOBILITY CHALLENGES	127
GROOMING DOGS WITH CHRONIC HEALTH CONDITIONS	128
GROOMING FOR DOGS WITH VISUAL OR HEARING IMPAIRMENTS	130
SHOW DOG GROOMING STANDARDS	131
THE IMPORTANCE OF SHOW DOG GROOMING	131
UNDERSTANDING THE BREED STANDARDS	132
GROOMING REQUIREMENTS FOR POPULAR SHOW BREEDS	133
SHOW DOG GROOMING TECHNIQUES	135
FINAL TOUCHES	136
CHAPTER 6: DIY GROOMING AT HOME	**138**
SETTING UP YOUR GROOMING SPACE	139
STEP-BY-STEP GROOMING ROUTINES	141
TROUBLESHOOTING COMMON GROOMING CHALLENGES	147
CHAPTER 7: PROFESSIONAL GROOMING	**154**
WHEN TO SEEK A PROFESSIONAL GROOMER	155
WHAT TO EXPECT DURING A PROFESSIONAL GROOMING SESSION	159
INITIAL CONSULTATION AND ASSESSMENT	160
BATHING AND CLEANING	160
BRUSHING AND COMB-OUT	161
NAIL TRIMMING AND PAW CARE	162
EAR CLEANING AND EYE CARE	163
COAT CLIPPING, TRIMMING, AND STYLING	163
FINAL TOUCHES AND CHECK-OUT	164
BUILDING A RELATIONSHIP WITH YOUR GROOMER	165
INITIAL MEETING AND CONSULTATION	165

Trust and Consistency	166
Open Communication	166
Understanding Grooming Limits and Preferences	167
Mutual Respect for Each Other's Role	168
Continued Education and Feedback	168
Building Long-Term Trust	169

CHAPTER 8: BREED-SPECIFIC GROOMING — 171

Popular Breeds and Their Unique Grooming Requirements	172
Labrador Retriever	172
Poodle	173
Shih Tzu	174
German Shepherd	174
Cocker Spaniel	175
Yorkshire Terrier	176
Border Collie	176
Bichon Frise	177
Dachshund	178
Tips for Mixed Breeds	179
Understanding the Coat Type of Your Mixed-Breed Dog	179
Creating a Regular Grooming Routine	180
Dealing with Shedding	182
Common Grooming Issues for Mixed Breeds	182
Dealing with Unique Grooming Needs	183
Grooming at Home vs. Professional Grooming	184

CHAPTER 9: ADVANCED TOPICS IN GROOMING — 186

Creative Grooming: Hair Dyeing and Accessories	187
Grooming as a Business: Starting a Career	191

FINAL THOUGHTS — 198

Grooming as a Bonding Experience	198

MAINTAINING A LIFETIME GROOMING ROUTINE   **199**
FAREWELL MESSAGE   **202**

Introduction

The Importance of Grooming for Your Dog's Health and Well-Being

Grooming is far more than a cosmetic endeavor; it is an essential component of responsible dog care. For many, grooming conjures images of sparkling coats and primped pups, but its significance extends beyond surface-level beauty. Grooming contributes to your dog's overall health, comfort, and emotional well-being. Whether you're brushing your dog's coat, trimming their nails, or cleaning their ears, every act of grooming serves as an opportunity to nurture their physical and emotional health.

In this section, we will explore the importance of grooming and how it impacts your dog's well-being across various dimensions.

Grooming and Physical Health

At its core, grooming plays a vital role in maintaining your dog's physical health. Regular grooming keeps your dog's coat clean and free of dirt, debris, and parasites. Beyond the aesthetics, grooming also provides an opportunity for early detection of potential health issues, making it a cornerstone of preventive care.

- **Skin and Coat Health:**
  The skin is your dog's largest organ, and its health is a direct reflection of your dog's overall well-being. Regular brushing not only removes dead hair but also stimulates the skin, improving blood circulation and promoting the production of natural oils. These oils keep the coat shiny and the skin hydrated, preventing dryness and flakiness.

Additionally, brushing helps to distribute these oils evenly across the coat, reducing the risk of matting and tangling. Mats, when left unchecked, can create painful pressure points on the skin and become breeding grounds for bacteria and parasites.

- **Parasite Prevention:**
Grooming sessions are the perfect opportunity to check your dog for parasites like fleas, ticks, and mites. These tiny invaders can cause itching, discomfort, and serious health problems if left untreated. By thoroughly inspecting your dog's coat during grooming, you can catch and address infestations early.
- **Ear and Eye Care:**
Cleaning your dog's ears is an essential part of grooming. Neglecting ear hygiene can lead to wax build-up, infections, and even hearing loss. Similarly, regular eye cleaning prevents tear stains and reduces the risk of eye infections caused by dirt or debris.
- **Nail and Paw Health:**
Overgrown nails can cause pain, difficulty walking, and even structural issues in your dog's posture. Grooming ensures nails are trimmed to a healthy length, preventing these problems. Paw pads, often overlooked, can also become cracked or sore without proper care, especially in extreme weather conditions.

Emotional and Behavioral Benefits of Grooming

Dogs are social animals that thrive on connection and routine. Grooming provides a unique opportunity for you to bond with your dog, building trust and strengthening your relationship.

- **A Bonding Experience:**
The time you spend grooming your dog is time spent nurturing your bond. The act of gently brushing their coat or massaging their paws reinforces their trust in you as their caregiver. This bond is particularly important for rescue dogs or those with a history of neglect, as it helps rebuild their confidence and sense of security.
- **Stress Reduction:**
Just as humans feel relaxed after a spa day, dogs also experience stress relief during grooming. When done in a calm and soothing manner, grooming can become a therapeutic experience for your dog, reducing anxiety and promoting a sense of well-being.
- **Training and Behavior:**
Grooming is an excellent way to familiarize your dog with being handled, which is crucial for veterinary visits and other situations where physical handling is necessary. Dogs that are regularly groomed are often more comfortable with human touch, making them less likely to exhibit fear-based behaviors.

Preventive Care Through Grooming

One of the most significant advantages of regular grooming is its role in preventive healthcare. Grooming allows you to detect abnormalities early, enabling prompt intervention and potentially saving your dog from more serious health issues.

- **Detecting Lumps and Bumps:**
While brushing or bathing your dog, you may come across lumps, bumps, or areas of sensitivity. Early detection of these changes can lead to a timely diagnosis and treatment,

whether it's a benign cyst or a more serious condition like cancer.
- **Monitoring Weight and Condition:**
Grooming sessions also allow you to assess your dog's body condition. You may notice weight loss, weight gain, or changes in muscle tone that warrant a closer look.
- **Spotting Skin Conditions:**
Regular grooming helps you identify skin conditions such as rashes, hot spots, or infections. These issues can often be managed effectively when caught early, preventing unnecessary discomfort for your dog.

Grooming as a Foundation for Lifelong Health

Grooming is not a one-time event but a lifelong practice that evolves with your dog's needs. Puppies require gentle introductions to grooming, while senior dogs may need extra care and attention due to mobility issues or medical conditions. By establishing a consistent grooming routine, you are investing in your dog's long-term health and happiness.

- **Puppy Grooming:**
Starting grooming early helps puppies become accustomed to the process, reducing stress as they grow. A gentle and patient approach during puppyhood lays the foundation for a lifetime of positive grooming experiences.
- **Senior Dog Grooming:**
As dogs age, their grooming needs change. Senior dogs may develop arthritis or other conditions that require careful handling. Grooming becomes not only a necessity but also a way to monitor their changing health needs.

Beyond the Basics: Grooming as a Lifestyle

For some dog owners, grooming becomes a hobby or even a profession. Whether you're aiming to enter your dog in shows or simply enjoy the satisfaction of a well-groomed pet, grooming offers endless opportunities for creativity and personal expression.

- **Show Grooming:**
  Competitive grooming requires advanced skills and an in-depth understanding of breed standards. While it demands dedication, it can also be incredibly rewarding.
- **Creative Grooming:**
  For those who love to experiment, creative grooming offers a chance to showcase your dog's personality through unique styles, trims, and accessories.

Grooming is much more than a routine chore; it is an integral part of your dog's care that touches every aspect of their health and well-being. By making grooming a priority, you not only enhance your dog's quality of life but also deepen the bond you share. With the right tools, knowledge, and techniques, grooming can transform from a mundane task into a joyful and rewarding experience for both you and your furry companion.

Chapter 1: Understanding Dog Grooming Basics

Dog grooming is an essential aspect of responsible pet care, yet it goes far beyond simply keeping your dog clean. At its core, grooming is a combination of science and art, requiring a deep understanding of your dog's unique needs, coat type, and overall health. For first-time pet owners and seasoned dog lovers alike, mastering the basics of grooming lays the foundation for ensuring your dog's well-being and comfort.

Every dog is unique, with grooming requirements that depend on factors such as their breed, coat type, lifestyle, and health conditions. From silky coats that demand daily brushing to wiry fur that needs regular trimming, understanding these individual needs is crucial. Additionally, grooming is about more than just the coat; it encompasses nail care, ear cleaning, dental hygiene, and even skincare.

This chapter provides an introduction to the fundamentals of dog grooming, exploring topics such as coat anatomy, different grooming tools, and safe handling practices. By grasping these basics, you'll be equipped with the knowledge to make grooming a positive experience for both you and your dog. Whether you're grooming at home or preparing for a visit to a professional, these foundational principles will guide you every step of the way.

The Anatomy of a Dog's Coat

Understanding the anatomy of a dog's coat is fundamental to mastering dog grooming. A dog's coat serves as more than just a visual indicator of breed or personality; it is a vital protective layer that regulates body temperature, shields the skin from harmful environmental factors, and even plays a role in communication.

The Structure of a Dog's Coat

A dog's coat consists of two primary layers: the outer coat (also known as the guard coat or topcoat) and the undercoat. Each layer has a specific function, and together, they form a system designed to protect and adapt to various environmental conditions.

- **The Outer Coat (Guard Coat):**
  The outer coat is made up of longer, coarser hairs that provide a shield against dirt, water, and UV radiation. These hairs are responsible for the overall texture and appearance of the coat. The outer coat also plays a role in repelling moisture, keeping the dog dry during light rain or snow.
- **The Undercoat:**
  The undercoat is softer, denser, and located beneath the outer coat. Its primary function is insulation, helping to regulate the dog's body temperature. In cold weather, the undercoat traps warm air close to the skin, while in hot weather, it provides a barrier against excessive heat. Dogs with a thick undercoat, such as Siberian Huskies, are especially well-adapted to cold climates.

Some breeds, such as Poodles or Maltese, lack a significant undercoat and are referred to as "single-coated" breeds. These dogs may require more frequent grooming since their coats grow continuously, making them prone to matting.

Coat Types and Textures

The texture and type of a dog's coat vary widely among breeds, each tailored to specific environmental or working conditions. Knowing your dog's coat type is essential for determining the best grooming practices.

- **Smooth Coats:**
  Smooth-coated dogs, such as Beagles and Boxers, have short, close-lying hair that requires minimal grooming. These coats are easy to maintain, but they still benefit from regular brushing to remove dead hair and distribute natural oils.
- **Double Coats:**
  Breeds like Golden Retrievers and German Shepherds have double coats, consisting of a dense undercoat and a longer outer coat. These coats are prone to seasonal shedding, especially during spring and fall when dogs "blow" their coats to prepare for temperature changes.
- **Wiry Coats:**
  Dogs with wiry coats, such as Terriers, have coarse, bristle-like hair that offers protection in rough environments. These coats require a grooming technique called hand-stripping to remove dead hairs and maintain the coat's texture.
- **Curly Coats:**
  Breeds like Poodles and Bichon Frises have curly, dense hair that grows continuously. These coats are highly prone to matting and require frequent brushing and trimming to stay manageable.

- **Silky Coats:**
  Silky-coated breeds, such as Yorkshire Terriers, have long, fine hair that resembles human hair. These coats demand regular grooming to prevent tangling and maintain their luxurious appearance.
- **Hairless Breeds:**
  Some breeds, like the Chinese Crested or Xoloitzcuintli, have little to no coat. These dogs require unique care, such as regular moisturizing and sun protection, to keep their skin healthy.

Coat Colors and Patterns

A dog's coat color and pattern are determined by genetics and can be a defining characteristic of their breed. While coat color may not directly affect grooming, understanding patterns can help identify areas that may require extra attention.

- **Solid Colors:**
  Solid-colored dogs, such as Labrador Retrievers, have a uniform coat color. Grooming for these dogs focuses on maintaining shine and removing loose hair.
- **Parti-Colored Coats:**
  Dogs with patches of two or more colors, like Border Collies, often have varied textures in their coat that may require different grooming approaches.
- **Brindle and Merle Patterns:**
  Unique patterns like brindle or merle add complexity to a dog's appearance but don't typically impact grooming requirements.

Seasonal Shedding and Coat Cycles

A dog's coat goes through natural cycles of growth, rest, and shedding. Understanding these cycles can help you plan grooming routines more effectively.

- **Anagen Phase:**
  This is the active growth phase of the coat. Dogs with continuously growing hair, such as Shih Tzus, remain in this phase for extended periods.
- **Catagen Phase:**
  During this transitional phase, hair growth slows, and the hair follicles prepare to enter a resting state.
- **Telogen Phase:**
  This is the resting phase of the coat cycle, during which the hair remains in place but is no longer growing.
- **Exogen Phase:**
  The shedding phase, during which old hairs are released to make way for new growth. This phase is most noticeable in double-coated breeds, particularly during seasonal shedding periods.

The Role of Natural Oils

The sebaceous glands in a dog's skin produce natural oils that keep the coat shiny and the skin moisturized. Regular brushing helps distribute these oils evenly across the coat, preventing dryness and improving its overall condition. Over-bathing can strip these oils, leading to dry skin and a dull coat, so it's important to balance cleanliness with the preservation of natural oils.

Common Coat-Related Issues

Several issues can arise if a dog's coat is not properly maintained. Regular grooming helps prevent and address these problems:

- **Matting:**
  Mats occur when hair becomes tangled and knotted. They can be painful for the dog and may even lead to skin infections.
- **Shedding:**
  While shedding is a natural process, excessive shedding may indicate underlying health issues such as poor diet or skin conditions.
- **Parasites:**
  Fleas, ticks, and mites can hide within a dog's coat, causing discomfort and potentially transmitting diseases.
- **Skin Irritations:**
  Allergies, dryness, and hot spots are common skin issues that can be detected early during grooming.

Grooming for Different Coat Types

Each coat type requires specific grooming techniques to maintain its health and appearance.

- **Short-Coated Breeds:**
  Use a bristle brush or grooming glove to remove loose hair and promote shine.
- **Long-Coated Breeds:**
  Regular brushing with a slicker brush or pin brush is essential to prevent tangling.
- **Curly-Coated Breeds:**
  Invest in detangling sprays and high-quality scissors for trimming.

- **Wiry-Coated Breeds:**
  Consider professional grooming for hand-stripping or specialized trimming.

The anatomy of a dog's coat is as diverse as the breeds themselves. Grooming is not just about aesthetics; it is a crucial aspect of your dog's overall well-being.

Different Coat Types and Their Grooming Needs

A dog's coat is one of its most distinguishing features, and understanding the unique characteristics of various coat types is crucial for providing proper grooming. Each type of coat serves a specific function, from protecting the dog in harsh environments to aiding in thermoregulation. However, these different coat types also come with distinct grooming requirements, which, if not met, can lead to discomfort, skin issues, and poor coat health. Whether you're dealing with a smooth coat or a dense double coat, tailoring your grooming routine to your dog's coat type ensures not only a healthy appearance but also overall well-being.

Smooth Coats

Smooth-coated dogs, such as Boxers, Doberman Pinschers, and Beagles, have short, sleek fur that lies close to the body. These coats are low-maintenance but still benefit from regular care to maintain their natural shine and remove loose hair.

Grooming Needs for Smooth Coats:

- Use a rubber grooming mitt or bristle brush to remove loose hairs and stimulate natural oil production in the skin.

- A monthly bath is generally sufficient, but more frequent bathing may be needed for dogs that get dirty outdoors.
- Pay attention to shedding seasons; while smooth-coated dogs may not shed as heavily as other breeds, they can still benefit from extra brushing during these times.

Double Coats

Double-coated breeds, such as Golden Retrievers, Siberian Huskies, and German Shepherds, have two distinct layers of fur: a dense, insulating undercoat and a protective outer coat. This combination provides excellent temperature regulation and weather resistance, but it also means these dogs are prone to heavy shedding, especially during seasonal changes.

Grooming Needs for Double Coats:

- Regular brushing with an undercoat rake or slicker brush is essential to remove loose undercoat hairs and prevent matting.
- During seasonal shedding, often referred to as "blowing their coat," increase brushing frequency to manage the large amount of loose fur.
- Avoid shaving double-coated dogs, as their coat layers are vital for regulating body temperature and protecting their skin.

Long Coats

Long-coated breeds, such as Afghan Hounds, Shih Tzus, and Yorkshire Terriers, have flowing, luxurious fur that requires consistent care to keep it tangle-free and healthy. These coats are often prone to matting, especially in areas prone to friction, like behind the ears or under the legs.

Grooming Needs for Long Coats:

- Daily brushing with a pin brush or slicker brush is necessary to prevent tangles and mats.
- Regular baths with a high-quality dog shampoo help keep the coat clean and shiny, followed by a conditioner to maintain softness.
- Long-coated dogs often require professional grooming for trimming or styling, especially for breeds with specific breed-standard cuts.

Curly Coats

Curly-coated breeds, such as Poodles, Portuguese Water Dogs, and Bichon Frises, have dense, curly hair that grows continuously. These coats are highly prone to matting if not properly maintained and require consistent grooming to keep them in top condition.

Grooming Needs for Curly Coats:

- Daily or every-other-day brushing with a slicker brush and detangling comb is essential to prevent mats.
- Regular trims, either at home or with a professional groomer, are necessary to manage the coat's length and prevent overgrowth.
- Use a moisturizing shampoo and conditioner during baths to prevent dryness and enhance the coat's texture.

Wire Coats

Wiry-coated breeds, such as Terriers, Schnauzers, and Irish Wolfhounds, have a coarse, bristle-like outer coat designed to repel dirt and protect the dog in rugged environments. These coats require specific grooming techniques to maintain their texture.

Grooming Needs for Wire Coats:

- Weekly brushing with a slicker brush or stripping knife helps remove loose hairs and maintain the coat's rough texture.
- Hand-stripping, a grooming technique where dead hairs are manually removed, is recommended for maintaining the coat's proper look and feel.
- Professional grooming may be needed for hand-stripping or specialized cuts required for certain breeds.

Silky Coats

Silky-coated breeds, such as Cocker Spaniels, Maltese, and Afghan Hounds, have fine, soft hair that requires regular care to prevent tangling and maintain its glossy appearance. These coats are particularly prone to becoming dirty or dull without consistent grooming.

Grooming Needs for Silky Coats:

- Daily brushing with a soft-bristle or pin brush helps maintain shine and prevent tangles.
- Use detangling sprays for stubborn knots, especially in areas prone to matting.
- Regular baths with a gentle shampoo are essential to keep the coat clean and soft.

Hairless Breeds

Hairless breeds, such as the Chinese Crested or the Xoloitzcuintli, lack a traditional coat but still require grooming attention to maintain their skin's health. These dogs are more prone to skin irritations, sunburn, and dryness due to the absence of protective fur.

Grooming Needs for Hairless Breeds:

- Regular moisturizing with a dog-safe lotion is essential to prevent dry skin.
- Sunscreen formulated for dogs should be applied before outdoor activities to protect against sunburn.
- Occasional bathing with a gentle shampoo helps remove dirt and maintain skin health.

Combination Coats

Some dogs, such as Border Collies and Australian Shepherds, have combination coats with areas of short fur and longer, feathered fur. These coats require a varied grooming approach to address the needs of different sections of the coat.

Grooming Needs for Combination Coats:

- Regular brushing with a slicker brush or pin brush to remove loose hairs and prevent tangles in feathered areas.
- Pay extra attention to the longer fur around the legs, tail, and chest, which is more prone to matting.
- Routine baths and careful drying ensure the coat stays clean and healthy.

Corded Coats

Corded coats, found in breeds like Komondors and Pulis, naturally form long, rope-like cords as the hair grows and mats together. These coats are highly unique and require specialized care to maintain their appearance and function.

Grooming Needs for Corded Coats:

- Separate cords regularly to prevent them from merging and forming large mats.
- Regular baths are necessary, but drying can take a long time; ensure the coat is completely dry to avoid mildew or odors.
- Professional grooming or advice from experienced owners may be needed to master cord care.

Shedding and Seasonal Considerations

Regardless of coat type, many dogs experience seasonal changes in their grooming needs. During shedding seasons, dogs may lose more hair as they adapt to temperature changes. Regular brushing, combined with proper nutrition, helps manage shedding and keeps the coat in top condition.

Tailoring Grooming to Your Dog's Needs

While understanding coat types provides a solid foundation, it's equally important to consider your dog's individual needs. Factors such as age, lifestyle, and health conditions may influence how often and in what way you groom your dog. By staying attuned to your dog's unique grooming requirements, you can ensure they remain healthy, comfortable, and looking their best.

Through consistent care and attention, you can enhance not only the appearance of your dog's coat but also their overall quality of life. Grooming is more than a task—it's an opportunity to bond and care for your furry companion.

Tools of the Trade: Brushes, Clippers, Scissors, and More

Grooming your dog is an essential part of maintaining its health and well-being, and to achieve the best results, you need the right tools for the job. Just like a skilled carpenter needs the proper tools to build a masterpiece, a dog groomer relies on a variety of grooming instruments to keep their dog's coat in top condition. Understanding what each tool does and how it contributes to the grooming process can help make your dog's grooming routine smoother and more effective. Whether you're new to dog grooming or you've been at it for years, a thorough understanding of the tools you're using is key to achieving the best possible outcome for your dog.

Each dog coat type and individual grooming requirement may require specific tools, and using the right one will not only make the job easier but also ensure that your dog is comfortable and that the grooming process is safe. Let's dive deep into the tools of the trade, from brushes to clippers, combs, and scissors, and learn how each one serves its purpose in the grooming process.

Brushes: Essential for Maintenance and Health

Brushing is one of the most fundamental parts of dog grooming. It helps to remove tangles, mats, and loose hair, distributes natural oils throughout the coat, and stimulates the skin. The right brush can make a huge difference in maintaining the health of your dog's coat.

Several types of brushes are designed for different coat types and grooming needs.

Bristle Brushes
Bristle brushes are typically used for dogs with short coats. These brushes have flexible bristles that are gentle on the skin and coat. They are ideal for smoothing out loose hairs, distributing oils, and adding a polished look to the dog's coat. These brushes can be used on smooth-coated breeds like Beagles, Boxers, and Dachshunds.

Slicker Brushes
Slicker brushes are equipped with fine, densely packed wire pins. They are highly effective at removing mats and tangles, especially in long-haired and double-coated breeds. Slicker brushes work well on dogs like Golden Retrievers, Poodles, and Shih Tzus. When using a slicker brush, care must be taken to avoid excessive pressure, as this can cause discomfort or irritation to your dog's skin.

Pin Brushes
Pin brushes are similar to slicker brushes but have softer, widely spaced pins. They are typically used for dogs with long, silky coats like Yorkshire Terriers, Afghan Hounds, and Maltese. Pin brushes help remove tangles and mats without damaging the coat, and they can be used to smooth and finish the coat for a glossy shine.

Rubber Brushes
Rubber brushes are designed for short-haired dogs or for use during shedding seasons. These brushes are often made of rubber bristles and are very effective at loosening and removing shedding fur. They are also great for massaging your dog's skin, promoting blood circulation. These brushes work well on breeds like Greyhounds, Beagles, and Boxers.

Undercoat Rakes

For double-coated dogs, such as Huskies and German Shepherds, undercoat rakes are essential tools for removing dense undercoat hairs. These tools have teeth designed to gently pull through the dense undercoat without damaging the topcoat. Regular use of an undercoat rake prevents matting and helps manage heavy seasonal shedding.

Clippers: Keeping the Coat Trimmed and Tidy

Dog clippers are indispensable for trimming and cutting hair. Different clippers are designed for different jobs, from simple trims to intricate styling. Choosing the right clipper is crucial for a smooth grooming experience and for your dog's safety.

Cordless Clippers

Cordless clippers are designed for ease of movement and flexibility. They are a great choice for dogs who don't sit still or for grooming in areas where access to a power outlet might be limited. Cordless clippers usually come with rechargeable batteries and can handle the cutting of most coat types. Brands like Wahl and Andis offer a variety of models suited for both professional and home use.

Corded Clippers

Corded clippers, unlike their cordless counterparts, require a constant power supply through an electrical cord. These clippers are usually more powerful and can be used for heavier-duty trimming, such as for thick or matted coats. They are an excellent choice for professional groomers and are ideal for breeds with dense or long fur, like Poodles, Schnauzers, and Terriers.

Clippers with Adjustable Blades

Clippers with adjustable blades allow you to choose from various cutting lengths, providing flexibility when grooming different areas of your dog's body. These are essential for dogs that require varied cutting lengths, such as when trimming around sensitive areas like the ears or paws while leaving the rest of the coat longer.

Teddy Bear Clippers

For certain breeds, particularly small dogs with fluffy, soft coats, teddy bear clippers provide a gentle cut that mimics the natural texture of their coat. These clippers help create a rounded, cute appearance without overly cutting the fur. Shih Tzus, Lhasa Apsos, and Bichon Frises often benefit from teddy bear clippers.

Scissors: Precision Grooming for a Flawless Look

While clippers are great for cutting large areas of fur quickly, scissors are often necessary for more detailed, precise work, such as trimming around the face, paws, ears, and tail. The right pair of scissors can make a significant difference in achieving a clean, polished look for your dog.

Straight Scissors

Straight scissors are commonly used for trimming the edges of the coat, especially for dogs with longer, straighter fur. They can be used to tidy up the coat's length or to trim around the eyes, ears, and paws. Straight scissors are particularly useful for breeds like Cocker Spaniels, Maltese, and Collies.

Curved Scissors

Curved scissors are designed to follow the natural contours of the dog's body. These scissors are ideal for shaping the dog's coat, especially around the legs, ears, and tail. The curvature allows for more precise cutting, creating natural-looking lines and helping to give the dog a professional, groomed appearance. Breeds like Poodles, Schnauzers, and Shih Tzus benefit from the use of curved scissors to maintain a neat look.

Thinning Shears

Thinning shears have teeth on one side of the blade and are designed for reducing bulk in thick, heavy coats. These shears are perfect for dogs with dense coats, such as German Shepherds and Huskies, as they help to lighten the coat and remove excess undercoat without affecting the overall length. Thinning shears are also used to blend and shape the coat, creating a more natural, less bulky appearance.

Combs: Detangling and Finishing Touches

Combs are useful for finishing a grooming session, especially for long-haired breeds prone to tangling. They can also be used to detangle small mats that may have formed while brushing.

Wide-Toothed Combs

Wide-toothed combs are essential for dogs with long, thick, or curly coats. They help to remove tangles without pulling on the hair. These combs are also great for use after applying conditioner during a bath, as they help distribute the product evenly and make detangling easier.

Fine-Toothed Combs

Fine-toothed combs are useful for dogs with silky, fine hair that requires extra detail in the grooming process. These combs can help with removing smaller mats, checking for pests like fleas, and tidying up the finer details of your dog's coat. They are often used for breeds like Maltese, Yorkies, and other fine-haired dogs.

Flea Combs

Flea combs are designed to remove fleas and other debris from your dog's coat. These combs have very fine, close-set teeth that catch fleas, flea eggs, and dirt, making it easier to manage flea infestations. Flea combs can be used in combination with other flea treatments for effective pest control.

Other Tools for a Complete Grooming Kit

While brushes, clippers, scissors, and combs are the main tools, several other accessories are useful in a well-rounded dog grooming toolkit.

Nail Clippers and Grinders

Trimming your dog's nails is an essential part of grooming. Nail clippers, such as scissor-style or guillotine clippers, are designed to safely trim the nails without cutting too far into the quick. Nail grinders, which use a rotating wheel to smooth the nail edges, are an excellent alternative for pets who are sensitive to traditional clippers.

Ear Cleaning Tools

For dogs prone to ear infections or wax buildup, ear cleaning tools such as ear wipes or sprays are essential for maintaining good ear hygiene. These tools help to remove debris, wax, and moisture, which could otherwise lead to infections.

Grooming Tables and Restraints

For convenience and comfort, a grooming table can help ensure that your dog is positioned at an optimal height for grooming. Restraints or grooming nooses can also be helpful in keeping your dog still during the grooming process, especially if your dog is fidgety or prone to moving around.

The right grooming tools can make a world of difference in both the ease and effectiveness of your dog's grooming routine. Always remember that regular grooming is an investment in your dog's overall health and well-being, and with the correct tools, it can also become a rewarding and enjoyable experience for both you and your pet.

Grooming Safety and Precautions

Grooming your dog is an essential part of maintaining its health, hygiene, and appearance. However, it's equally important to prioritize safety during the grooming process to prevent injuries and make the experience as comfortable as possible for your dog. Whether you are grooming your dog at home or taking it to a professional groomer, understanding the precautions necessary for each step of the grooming process is vital to ensure both the dog's well-being and your own.

While grooming is a routine task for many pet owners, it involves the use of tools that can potentially cause harm if not used correctly. Clippers, scissors, brushes, and other grooming tools can easily become a source of injury or discomfort for your dog if not handled carefully. Additionally, some dogs may become anxious or stressed during grooming, which can make the process even more challenging. Knowing how to handle your dog properly, using the correct tools, and paying attention to details will make grooming safer and more enjoyable for both of you.

In this section, we will explore the essential safety practices and precautions to take when grooming your dog. From handling sensitive areas to ensuring proper tool usage and maintaining a calm grooming environment, the following tips and recommendations will help you avoid accidents, ensure your dog's safety, and maintain a positive grooming experience.

Handling Your Dog During Grooming

Before even beginning the grooming process, it is crucial to create a calm and controlled environment. If your dog is anxious or easily excitable, it can be challenging to groom them effectively and safely. Taking the time to ensure your dog is properly handled during grooming will set the tone for the entire session.

Start Slow and Build Trust
If you're new to grooming or your dog is nervous, start with short grooming sessions to help build trust and comfort. Allow your dog to become familiar with the tools by showing them gently without actually using them at first. Give your dog time to get used to the sensation of being brushed or touched with grooming tools, especially in sensitive areas. Gradually introduce more advanced grooming steps like clipping or scissoring as your dog becomes more accustomed to the process.

Use Positive Reinforcement
Positive reinforcement is one of the most effective ways to ensure your dog's safety and cooperation during grooming. Reward your dog with treats, praise, or toys when they remain calm and follow directions. This will help create a positive association with grooming, which will make future grooming sessions easier for both

of you. Avoid scolding or punishing your dog, as this can increase anxiety and resistance.

Secure Your Dog Properly

Proper restraint is important, especially if your dog is squirming or anxious. Use a grooming table or a flat, non-slippery surface to keep your dog stable. If your dog is large or particularly squirmy, consider using a grooming restraint or leash to ensure they stay still. Be mindful not to use too much force to restrain your dog, as this can lead to stress or injury. Always make sure that the restraint does not hurt or restrict your dog's breathing.

Check for Health Issues

Before you begin grooming, take a moment to check your dog's body for any health concerns. Look for cuts, rashes, skin irritations, or signs of infection. If your dog has any health issues, such as ear infections or skin conditions, it may be wise to consult a veterinarian before proceeding with grooming. Grooming should never be done on irritated skin or infected areas, as this can exacerbate the problem and cause further discomfort to your dog.

Using the Right Tools Safely

One of the most critical aspects of grooming safely is ensuring you use the correct tools for the job and that they are in good condition. Using improper or blunt tools can cause injury to your dog, and it may make the grooming process less effective and more stressful for them.

Keep Tools Clean and Sharpened

Before each grooming session, check your tools for wear and tear. Clippers, scissors, and razors should all be sharp and clean. Dull tools can cause pain or discomfort when used on your dog's coat and may result in the hair being pulled rather than cut. Regularly clean and sanitize your grooming tools after each use to prevent the spread of bacteria and infection, especially when grooming dogs with skin issues or sensitivities.

Clippers and Blades
Clippers should be used with care to avoid cutting your dog's skin. Ensure the blades are not too hot by allowing them to cool down during breaks to prevent burns. When using clippers, always work in the direction of hair growth to minimize pulling and discomfort. Start with slow, gentle strokes to avoid startling your dog, and if your dog becomes agitated, stop and try again later. Clippers should never be used on areas like the face, eyes, or ears without a steady hand, and extra caution should be taken in these sensitive spots.

Scissors and Shears
When using scissors or shears, ensure they are properly sharpened and designed for dog grooming. Blunt scissors can cause frustration and discomfort, and they increase the risk of cutting your dog's skin. Always work in small sections, particularly around sensitive areas like the eyes, ears, and paws. Avoid using regular household scissors on your dog's coat, as they may not be designed to handle thicker or matted hair. Use curved scissors for better control, especially when trimming around the dog's face and body contours.

Brushes and Combs
When brushing, always use brushes appropriate for your dog's coat type. Too stiff a bristle can irritate a sensitive dog's skin, while brushes meant for long-haired dogs can be too rough for short-haired dogs. Always work gently to remove tangles or mats, and never yank or pull the hair. If your dog becomes uncomfortable or stressed,

take a break. Mats and tangles can be painful, so use a detangling spray or conditioner for easier brushing if necessary.

Grooming Sensitive Areas Safely

Certain areas of your dog's body are more delicate and require extra care when grooming. These areas are often more sensitive and may cause your dog pain if not handled correctly. Understanding how to safely groom these regions is essential to keeping your dog comfortable during the process.

Eyes
When grooming near your dog's eyes, take care to avoid causing injury. The skin around the eyes is thin and sensitive, so always use a gentle, soft brush or a fine-toothed comb to avoid causing irritation. If you need to trim hair around the eyes, use blunt-nosed scissors or specialized scissors designed for the face area. Be extremely cautious to avoid accidentally poking or irritating your dog's eyes.

Ears
Cleaning your dog's ears requires attention and care to avoid damaging the ear canal. Use an ear cleaner recommended by your veterinarian, and avoid sticking cotton swabs or fingers too far into the ear canal. Dogs with floppy ears, such as Cocker Spaniels or Basset Hounds, are more prone to ear infections, so be especially gentle when grooming these areas. If your dog's ears appear red, inflamed, or have an unusual odor, consult your veterinarian before continuing grooming.

Paws and Nail Care
Nail trimming can be one of the most challenging parts of grooming,

particularly if your dog is nervous or if the nails are too long. Use proper nail clippers designed for dogs, and be careful not to cut too close to the quick (the pink part inside the nail that contains blood vessels). Cutting too short can cause bleeding and pain. If you're unsure, consult a professional groomer for guidance.

Tail and Hindquarters
When grooming around your dog's tail or hindquarters, be mindful of their comfort. Some dogs can be sensitive around their back end, so go slow and pay attention to your dog's reactions. For long-haired dogs, gently brush the tail and rear to remove tangles. If trimming is necessary, use scissors with a rounded tip to avoid causing any accidental cuts.

Recognizing Signs of Stress or Discomfort

During the grooming process, it's important to watch for signs of stress or discomfort. Some dogs may show signs of anxiety or fear, especially if they are not accustomed to grooming. Recognizing these signs early can help you stop the grooming process before your dog becomes too stressed or hurt.

Signs of Stress

- Whining, growling, or barking
- Panting heavily or drooling excessively
- Attempting to escape or run away
- Flinching or pulling away from grooming tools
- Aggression or biting at the tools or you

If you notice any of these signs, it's essential to stop grooming immediately and give your dog a break. Take a step back, allow them to calm down, and resume when they are ready. If your dog is regularly stressed during grooming, consider consulting a professional groomer or veterinarian to address the issue and ensure a positive grooming experience in the future.

Safety during dog grooming is essential for both you and your pet. By following these precautions, using the proper tools, and taking extra care with sensitive areas, you can minimize the risks and make grooming a positive and enjoyable experience.

Chapter 2: Bathing and Hygiene

Bathing is a fundamental part of a dog's grooming routine that goes beyond keeping your pet clean and fresh. It plays a vital role in maintaining your dog's skin health, preventing infections, and ensuring overall well-being.

Understanding the right techniques, frequency, and products for your dog's bath is essential to avoid potential skin irritations or discomfort. In this chapter, we will explore the importance of proper bathing and hygiene, the different products available, and how to tailor the bathing process to suit your dog's specific needs.

Bathing not only removes dirt, allergens, and bacteria from your dog's coat, but it also helps manage odors and supports healthy skin by eliminating oils and buildup that can clog pores.

However, over-bathing or using inappropriate products can lead to dryness, irritation, or allergic reactions. It's important to choose the right dog shampoo for your pet's coat type, skin condition, and any sensitivities.

Additionally, hygiene extends beyond just a bath; it includes oral care, ear cleaning, and proper nail trimming. These routines work together to promote overall health and comfort for your dog. In this chapter, we will guide you through each step of proper bathing and hygiene practices, ensuring that your dog stays healthy, clean, and happy.

When and How to Bathe Your Dog

Bathing your dog is an essential part of its grooming routine, contributing to its overall health and well-being. However, understanding when to bathe your dog and the best techniques to use during the bath can significantly impact both the comfort of your dog and the effectiveness of the grooming process. Bathing too frequently or improperly can lead to skin irritations, dryness, and other health issues. On the other hand, infrequent bathing may result in an accumulation of dirt, oil, and odor, which can negatively affect your dog's coat and skin health. This section will guide you through the critical factors in determining when to bathe your dog and provide a step-by-step approach to bathing your dog safely and effectively.

When to Bathe Your Dog

The frequency of bathing largely depends on your dog's coat type, activity level, and health status. While there is no one-size-fits-all answer, there are a few general guidelines that can help you decide when your dog needs a bath.

Coat Type
Different coat types require different bathing schedules. Dogs with short coats, like Beagles or Dachshunds, typically require fewer baths than dogs with long or double coats, such as Golden Retrievers or Siberian Huskies. Short-haired dogs may only need a bath every 4 to 6 weeks, while long-haired dogs could benefit from more frequent bathing, especially if they get dirty more easily. Dogs with thick or double coats, such as Collies, may need baths every 6 to 8 weeks, depending on their grooming needs.

Activity Level

If your dog spends a lot of time outdoors, playing in dirt, mud, or water, it will require more frequent baths. Dogs that enjoy outdoor activities, like hiking, running, or playing fetch, tend to get dirtier faster and may need a bath once every few weeks. On the other hand, a dog that is mostly indoors and not exposed to dirt will need fewer baths. Keep an eye on your dog's coat for signs of dirt buildup or odors that may indicate it's time for a bath.

Skin Conditions and Allergies

Dogs with skin conditions, such as dry skin, rashes, hot spots, or fungal infections, may require special bathing schedules and products. If your dog has been diagnosed with a skin condition, your veterinarian may recommend medicated shampoos or more frequent baths to treat the condition. Always follow your vet's instructions when it comes to bathing dogs with skin sensitivities or allergies.

Odor and Dirt Buildup

An essential factor in deciding when to bathe your dog is odor. If your dog's coat starts to develop a strong odor or feels oily to the touch, it's a sign that it's time for a bath. Odors usually indicate that bacteria, dirt, and oils have built up in the coat, which can lead to skin issues if left unchecked. Regular baths will help maintain a fresh-smelling coat and prevent potential skin problems.

Puppies and Older Dogs

Puppies generally don't need frequent baths unless they get into something particularly dirty or smelly. Overbathing puppies can dry out their sensitive skin, so it's best to limit baths to when necessary. Older dogs, particularly those with mobility issues or health conditions, may also need special attention when it comes to bathing. If your senior dog doesn't get dirty often, it may not need frequent baths, but you should still monitor its hygiene and consult your vet for specific needs.

How to Bathe Your Dog

Bathing your dog should be a positive and enjoyable experience for both you and your pet. Proper technique and using the right products can make the process more efficient, reduce stress for your dog, and ensure that you're achieving the desired results. Here is a detailed, step-by-step guide to properly bathing your dog.

1. Gather Your Supplies

Before you begin, make sure you have everything you need for the bath to avoid interruptions during the process. Here's a checklist of supplies you should gather:

- Dog shampoo (choose one suitable for your dog's coat type and skin sensitivity)
- A towel or two (for drying your dog)
- A brush or comb (to remove tangles before the bath)
- A cup or pitcher for rinsing
- A detachable shower head or hose (if available)
- Cotton balls (for ear cleaning, if needed)
- Nail clippers (for trimming nails, if required)
- Dog conditioner (optional, for long-haired or dry-coated dogs)
- Dog toothbrush and toothpaste (for oral care during the bath)

2. Prepare the Bath Area

The location of the bath is important. You can bathe your dog in a bathtub, shower, or even outdoors using a garden hose (if the weather is suitable). Ensure the area is safe and non-slippery for your dog. Place a non-slip mat in the bathtub or shower to help your dog feel secure and prevent slipping.

If you're using a bathtub, consider placing a towel or blanket on the bottom to make your dog feel more comfortable. Make sure the water temperature is lukewarm, as hot or cold water can cause discomfort for your dog.

3. Brush Your Dog Before Bathing

Before getting your dog wet, it's important to brush its coat thoroughly. Brushing helps remove tangles, mats, and loose fur, which can become more difficult to manage once your dog is wet. Brushing also helps distribute the natural oils in your dog's coat, making the bathing process more effective. Be gentle around sensitive areas, like the ears and tail, to avoid causing discomfort.

4. Wet Your Dog's Coat

Gently wet your dog's coat with lukewarm water using a cup, pitcher, or detachable shower head. Start from the neck down and avoid getting water in your dog's ears, eyes, or nose. For dogs with longer or thicker coats, you may need to spend a little extra time thoroughly wetting the fur to ensure the shampoo works effectively. Keep the water pressure low and be gentle so that your dog remains calm throughout the process.

5. Apply Dog Shampoo

Once your dog's coat is thoroughly wet, apply a small amount of dog shampoo to their body, beginning at the neck and working your way down to the tail and legs. Massage the shampoo into your dog's coat with your fingers, creating a gentle lather. Be sure to cover the entire coat, but avoid the face and eyes. Use your hands or a soft sponge to lather up the shampoo in a circular motion, paying special attention to areas that tend to accumulate dirt or oils, such as the paws, underarms, and belly.

6. Rinse Thoroughly

After massaging the shampoo into your dog's coat, it's time to rinse. Use lukewarm water to rinse out all of the shampoo. This step is crucial to prevent shampoo residue from irritating your dog's skin. Rinse until the water runs clear, ensuring that no product is left behind. Take your time during this step, as leftover shampoo can cause itching, dryness, and discomfort.

7. Optional: Use Conditioner

For dogs with long or dry coats, you may want to use a conditioner to help nourish their skin and coat. Apply a small amount of conditioner, massage it into the coat, and leave it in for a few minutes before rinsing thoroughly. Be sure to choose a conditioner that is specifically designed for dogs, as human conditioners may contain ingredients that are harmful to pets.

8. Drying Your Dog

Once the bath is complete, gently towel-dry your dog to remove excess water. Use a soft towel and pat rather than rub to avoid tangling or irritating your dog's coat. If your dog has a thick or long coat, you may need to use a blow dryer on a low, cool setting to help speed up the drying process. Keep the dryer a few inches away from your dog's skin to avoid burns or discomfort. If your dog is nervous about the dryer, consider air drying or using a towel to soak up most of the moisture.

9. Ear Cleaning

If necessary, take a moment to clean your dog's ears during or after the bath. Dogs with floppy ears or excess wax buildup may require more frequent ear cleaning. Use a dog-safe ear cleaner and a cotton ball to gently wipe the outer parts of the ear. Avoid inserting anything into the ear canal to prevent injury.

10. Nail Trimming

If your dog's nails are getting long, you can also use bath time as an opportunity to trim its nails. Make sure to use proper nail clippers designed for dogs, and avoid cutting too close to the quick. If you're unsure how to trim your dog's nails, it's a good idea to ask your vet or groomer for guidance.

Aftercare and Final Tips

After the bath, monitor your dog for any signs of irritation, such as excessive scratching, redness, or dryness. If you notice any unusual reactions, it's important to consult your veterinarian.

Remember that consistency is key to keeping your dog clean, comfortable, and healthy. Bathing is just one part of your dog's grooming routine, so make sure to also incorporate regular brushing, ear cleaning, and nail trimming into their care schedule. By bathing your dog correctly, at the right frequency, and with the right products, you'll help ensure that your dog's coat and skin remain healthy and vibrant for years to come.

Selecting the Right Shampoos and Conditioners

When it comes to dog grooming, selecting the right shampoo and conditioner is one of the most important decisions you will make for your pet's health and appearance. Not all shampoos and conditioners are created equal, and using the wrong products can lead to skin irritations, dryness, or other dermatological issues. It's essential to understand your dog's specific coat type, skin condition, and grooming needs before choosing the products that will best serve them. In this section, we will explore how to select the right shampoos and conditioners for your dog, how to use them effectively, and the differences between various formulations.

Understanding Your Dog's Skin and Coat Type

Before selecting a shampoo or conditioner, it is crucial to understand the specifics of your dog's skin and coat. Just like humans, dogs have different skin types and coat types, each of which may require different grooming products. Understanding your dog's skin condition, coat texture, and overall health will help you choose the most appropriate shampoo and conditioner.

Skin Type

Dog skin types vary just as much as human skin types. There are generally three categories of skin type:

- **Normal skin:** Dogs with normal skin are healthy and have no major skin issues. They don't experience excessive dryness or oiliness. Dogs with normal skin typically don't require medicated or specialty shampoos, and you can use standard gentle shampoos to maintain their skin health.
- **Dry skin:** Dry, flaky, or itchy skin is common in dogs with longer coats or those exposed to harsh environmental factors. These dogs may benefit from moisturizing shampoos and conditioners that contain hydrating ingredients such as aloe vera or oatmeal. Using a product specifically formulated for dry skin can help soothe irritation and provide the necessary moisture.

- **Oily skin:** Some dogs, especially those with certain breeds, may have naturally oily skin. If your dog's skin becomes greasy or emits an unpleasant odor between baths, an oil-controlling shampoo may be required. Look for shampoos designed for oily skin that can remove excess oils without stripping the skin of its essential moisture.
- **Sensitive skin:** Dogs with sensitive skin are prone to irritation or allergic reactions. This is especially true for breeds that have more delicate skin, such as Greyhounds, Whippets, or Chihuahuas. If your dog suffers from rashes, redness, or itchiness after a bath, a hypoallergenic, fragrance-free shampoo is your best option. These products are specially formulated to be gentle on sensitive skin without causing further irritation.

Coat Type

The texture of your dog's coat also determines the type of shampoo and conditioner that will work best. Understanding your dog's coat type will ensure that you are using products that suit its specific grooming needs.

- **Short coats:** Dogs with short coats, such as Boxers, Beagles, or Dachshunds, generally require less maintenance than long-haired breeds. These dogs typically don't need heavy conditioning but may benefit from a gentle shampoo that cleans and nourishes the coat without weighing it down. Some short-haired dogs may have more sensitive skin, so a moisturizing or soothing shampoo could be beneficial.
- **Long or silky coats:** Breeds like Yorkies, Shih Tzus, and Afghan Hounds with long, silky coats require more attention to prevent tangling, matting, and dryness. Long coats often require conditioning products that moisturize, detangle, and

add shine. Conditioners can also make brushing easier by softening the fur and preventing static buildup.
- **Double coats:** Breeds like Huskies, German Shepherds, and Golden Retrievers have double coats, which include a dense undercoat and a topcoat. Double-coated dogs shed heavily, and regular grooming is essential to keep their coats in good condition. Special shampoos for double coats typically remove loose undercoat hair, control shedding, and help prevent matting. These shampoos often include ingredients that improve the texture and manageability of both layers of the coat.
- **Curly or wavy coats:** Dogs like Poodles, Bichon Frises, and Portuguese Water Dogs have curly or wavy coats that require extra care to prevent tangles and mats. These coats can become easily dry and frizzy, so it's important to use moisturizing shampoos and conditioners designed to hydrate and smooth the fur. Look for products that add definition to the curls and leave the coat soft and manageable.

Key Ingredients to Look for in Dog Shampoos and Conditioners

Different ingredients in dog shampoos and conditioners serve various purposes. When choosing the right products, consider the following key ingredients based on your dog's skin and coat needs:

1. **Oatmeal:**
Oatmeal is a soothing ingredient that is commonly found in shampoos designed for dogs with dry or itchy skin. Oatmeal helps relieve irritation, reduce redness, and lock moisture into the skin. It is also gentle and can be used regularly without causing further sensitivity.

2. Aloe Vera:

Aloe vera is another popular ingredient known for its soothing and healing properties. It can help to calm irritated skin and reduce itching and inflammation. Aloe-based shampoos and conditioners are ideal for dogs with dry, flaky, or sensitive skin.

3. Tea Tree Oil:

Tea tree oil has natural antiseptic properties that can help cleanse the skin and prevent infections. It is often used in shampoos formulated for dogs with fungal or bacterial skin infections. However, it is essential to ensure that tea tree oil is diluted properly, as high concentrations can be toxic to dogs.

4. Chamomile:

Chamomile is a calming ingredient that helps to soothe inflamed or irritated skin. It is often used in shampoos for dogs with allergies or those experiencing mild skin conditions. Chamomile also has a pleasant fragrance that can help neutralize odors.

5. Omega Fatty Acids (Omega-3 and Omega-6):

Omega fatty acids are crucial for maintaining healthy skin and coat. They help reduce inflammation, maintain moisture, and promote the growth of a shiny, healthy coat. Omega fatty acids are often included in shampoos and conditioners for dogs with dry or dull coats.

6. Coconut Oil:

Coconut oil is a natural moisturizer that helps to nourish the skin and coat. It has antimicrobial properties, making it ideal for preventing skin infections. Coconut oil-based shampoos are perfect for dry or flaky skin, as they provide deep hydration and shine.

7. Essential   Oils:
Essential oils, like lavender and eucalyptus, are commonly found in dog grooming products. They provide a soothing aroma and can help relax both you and your dog during bath time. However, it's important to ensure that the essential oils used are dog-safe, as some can be harmful to pets when used improperly.

Types of Dog Shampoos and Conditioners

Now that you know what to look for in ingredients, it's important to choose the right type of shampoo and conditioner for your dog's specific needs. Below are some of the most common types of dog shampoos and conditioners and their uses.

1.   Medicated   Shampoos
Medicated shampoos are formulated to treat specific skin conditions, such as fungal infections, bacterial infections, hot spots, or allergies. If your dog has been diagnosed with a skin condition, your veterinarian may recommend a medicated shampoo. These products contain active ingredients like chlorhexidine, ketoconazole, or benzoyl peroxide, which target the cause of the skin issue. Medicated shampoos should only be used as directed by your vet, as they can be harsh if overused.

2.   Flea   and   Tick   Shampoos
Flea and tick shampoos are designed to eliminate fleas, ticks, and other external parasites. These shampoos typically contain insecticides or natural ingredients like pyrethrin to kill fleas and ticks on contact. While flea and tick shampoos are effective, they should be used in conjunction with other parasite control measures, such as oral or topical treatments.

3. Hypoallergenic Shampoos

Hypoallergenic shampoos are specially formulated for dogs with sensitive skin or allergies. These shampoos are free from harsh chemicals, fragrances, and dyes that could irritate the skin. They are ideal for dogs prone to itching, redness, or allergic reactions.

4. Deodorizing Shampoos

Deodorizing shampoos are designed to neutralize odors in your dog's coat. These shampoos often contain ingredients that eliminate bacteria and odors while leaving a fresh, clean scent. Deodorizing shampoos are a great option for dogs that have a strong natural odor or who have rolled in something unpleasant.

5. Moisturizing Shampoos

Moisturizing shampoos are ideal for dogs with dry or flaky skin. These shampoos are enriched with hydrating ingredients, such as oatmeal, aloe vera, or coconut oil, that help replenish moisture and restore the natural oils in the skin and coat.

6. Tearless Shampoos

Tearless shampoos are formulated to be gentle on your dog's face and eyes. These shampoos are perfect for puppies or older dogs who may be sensitive around their face. Tearless shampoos can clean without causing discomfort if they accidentally come into contact with your dog's eyes.

7. Detangling Conditioners

If your dog has long or curly hair, a detangling conditioner is an essential part of your grooming routine. These conditioners help to loosen tangles and prevent mats from forming, making it easier to brush your dog's coat. Detangling conditioners are ideal for breeds like Poodles, Shih Tzus, and other dogs with long, curly coats.

Choosing the right shampoo and conditioner for your dog is vital to their health and happiness. Whether your dog has dry, oily, sensitive skin, or a luxurious coat that needs special attention, the right grooming products can make a significant difference.

Cleaning Ears, Eyes, and Teeth

Maintaining proper hygiene for your dog goes beyond just bathing and grooming its coat. The ears, eyes, and teeth are essential parts of your dog's body that require regular care and attention. Without proper cleaning and maintenance, these areas can become prone to infections, irritation, and discomfort, which could affect your dog's overall health and well-being. This section will guide you through the importance of cleaning your dog's ears, eyes, and teeth, how to do it safely, and which products to use for each task.

Cleaning Your Dog's Ears

Your dog's ears are prone to dirt, moisture, and wax buildup, especially in certain breeds. Whether your dog has floppy ears or upright ones, ear hygiene is crucial to prevent ear infections, odor, and discomfort.

Why Cleaning Your Dog's Ears is Important

Dogs' ears are highly sensitive, and their shape can make it difficult for air to circulate properly, leading to an environment where bacteria, yeast, and moisture can thrive. Regular ear cleaning helps reduce the chances of infections, alleviates discomfort, and prevents wax buildup, which can cause hearing problems. Some dogs, especially those with long, floppy ears like Cocker Spaniels, Basset

Hounds, and Dachshunds, are more prone to ear infections because their ears trap moisture.

Signs Your Dog Needs Ear Cleaning

- Excessive scratching or pawing at their ears
- Foul odor emanating from the ears
- Redness or swelling in the ear canal
- Discharge, which could be yellow, brown, or black in color
- Rubbing their face on the ground or furniture

If your dog shows any of these signs, it's a good idea to check their ears and clean them as necessary. However, if you notice signs of infection, such as pus or blood, consult a veterinarian before cleaning the ears, as you may need professional care.

How to Clean Your Dog's Ears Safely

1. **Prepare the Cleaning Solution**: Choose an ear cleaning solution that is specifically formulated for dogs. These solutions are gentle and will not irritate the ear canal. Never use hydrogen peroxide, alcohol, or any harsh chemicals on your dog's ears, as they can cause irritation or damage to the sensitive skin inside the ear.
2. **Position Your Dog Comfortably**: It's important to make your dog feel calm and comfortable during the cleaning process. You can either have them lie down or sit in a relaxed position. If your dog is anxious, it may help to have someone assist you by holding them gently.
3. **Apply the Cleaning Solution**: Gently lift your dog's ear flap and apply the ear cleaning solution into the ear canal. Do not squirt the solution directly into the ear too forcefully,

as it can be uncomfortable. Follow the instructions on the product for the correct amount to use.
4. **Massage the Ear Base**: After applying the solution, gently massage the base of the ear to help loosen any dirt or wax. This can also help distribute the cleaner throughout the ear canal.
5. **Wipe the Ear Clean**: After massaging, let your dog shake their head to loosen the debris. Then, use a cotton ball or gauze pad to wipe away any remaining debris from the ear canal and ear flap. Do not insert the cotton ball deep into the ear canal, as this could cause injury or push debris further in.
6. **Repeat the Process**: Depending on the buildup of wax and dirt, you may need to clean your dog's ears weekly, or as recommended by your veterinarian.

Cleaning Your Dog's Eyes

Your dog's eyes are highly sensitive and require regular care to maintain good vision and prevent eye-related problems. Some breeds, especially those with prominent eyes like Bulldogs, Pugs, and Shih Tzus, are more prone to eye infections, discharge, and irritation. Regular eye cleaning will help prevent problems and keep your dog comfortable.

Why Cleaning Your Dog's Eyes is Important

Eye care is essential to prevent the buildup of tears, mucus, or dirt that can lead to eye infections or irritation. Dogs' eyes are also susceptible to injury from environmental factors like dust, pollen, and debris. In some breeds, tear staining can also occur, which is not only a health concern but can also affect your dog's appearance.

Signs Your Dog Needs Eye Cleaning

- Excessive tearing or watery eyes
- Redness or swelling around the eyes
- Thick, yellowish, or green discharge from the eyes
- Squinting, pawing at the eyes, or rubbing the face
- Tear stains beneath the eyes, especially in light-colored dogs

If you notice any of these symptoms, it may indicate a need for eye cleaning. In cases where there is significant discharge or infection, consult your veterinarian for further treatment.

How to Clean Your Dog's Eyes Safely

1. **Prepare the Right Cleaning Solution**: Use a gentle, dog-safe eye cleaning solution, which is usually available in liquid or wipe form. Make sure the solution is designed for pets and free of alcohol or other harsh chemicals.
2. **Restrain Your Dog Comfortably**: Gently hold your dog's head still by cupping their chin and keeping their body relaxed. You can also have someone else assist you by holding your dog while you clean their eyes.
3. **Apply the Solution**: If you're using eye wipes, gently wipe the area around the eyes to remove any dirt, debris, or discharge. If you're using a liquid solution, apply a few drops directly onto the eye area. Be sure to wipe away any discharge around the eye with a clean cotton ball or gauze pad.
4. **Wipe the Eyes Gently**: Always wipe from the corner of the eye outward. If your dog has tear stains, wipe the stained area gently to avoid further irritation. Use a separate cotton ball or pad for each eye to avoid cross-contamination.

5. **Repeat as Needed**: Depending on your dog's needs, clean their eyes once or twice a week or more frequently if they have persistent discharge or tear stains.

Cleaning Your Dog's Teeth

Dental hygiene is just as important for dogs as it is for humans. Poor oral hygiene can lead to bad breath, gum disease, tooth decay, and other serious health issues. Brushing your dog's teeth regularly will help prevent plaque buildup, tartar formation, and gum infections.

Why Cleaning Your Dog's Teeth is Important

Dogs can develop dental problems such as gingivitis, periodontitis, and tooth decay, which can cause pain, tooth loss, and even systemic infections. Regular teeth cleaning is essential to maintain healthy gums and teeth. It also helps to keep your dog's breath fresh and prevent unpleasant odors from developing.

Signs Your Dog Needs Teeth Cleaning

- Foul-smelling breath
- Red or swollen gums
- Excessive drooling
- Difficulty eating or chewing
- Yellow or brown tartar buildup on the teeth
- Bleeding gums

If your dog exhibits any of these signs, it may indicate the need for a more thorough dental cleaning, either at home or through professional care by a veterinarian.

How to Clean Your Dog's Teeth Safely

1. **Get the Right Tools**: Use a toothbrush and toothpaste designed specifically for dogs. Never use human toothpaste, as it contains ingredients that are harmful to dogs if swallowed. You can find dog-friendly toothbrushes in various sizes and shapes, including finger brushes or long-handled brushes that can reach the back teeth.
2. **Introduce Your Dog to Brushing Gradually**: If your dog is new to teeth brushing, take time to introduce the process slowly. Start by letting them sniff and lick the toothpaste so they become accustomed to the taste. Then, gently massage their gums with your finger before progressing to using the toothbrush.
3. **Brush in a Gentle, Circular Motion**: Apply a small amount of dog toothpaste to the brush, and gently brush your dog's teeth using circular motions. Focus on the outer surfaces of the teeth and gums, as this is where plaque and tartar tend to build up the most. Start slowly and gently, and gradually increase the amount of time you spend brushing as your dog becomes more comfortable with the process.
4. **Use Dental Chews and Toys**: In addition to regular brushing, you can also provide your dog with dental chews and toys that help remove plaque and tartar naturally. These can be especially helpful for dogs who are reluctant to have their teeth brushed.
5. **Consider Professional Dental Cleanings**: While home care is essential, regular professional dental cleanings by a veterinarian are also important, especially for dogs prone to dental problems. Professional cleanings remove tartar buildup that cannot be addressed by brushing alone.

Cleaning your dog's ears, eyes, and teeth is a crucial part of their grooming routine. These areas are often overlooked, but their hygiene plays a significant role in maintaining overall health and preventing infections or discomfort.

Managing Shedding and Dander

Dealing with shedding and dander is one of the most common challenges that dog owners face. While shedding is a natural process for most dogs, the amount of hair and the presence of dander can sometimes be overwhelming, especially for individuals with allergies. Understanding how shedding and dander work, along with adopting proper grooming practices and environmental management, can significantly reduce the impact of these issues. This section will dive deep into the causes of shedding, how to manage it, and practical solutions to minimize dander in your home.

Understanding Shedding in Dogs

Shedding is a normal biological process that all dogs go through at some point. Dogs shed their hair to get rid of old, damaged, or unwanted fur, making way for new growth. The frequency and intensity of shedding depend on several factors, including breed, health, environment, and season.

Why Do Dogs Shed?

1. **Seasonal Shedding**: Many dogs shed more in the spring and fall as their coats adjust to the changing weather. In spring, dogs typically shed their thicker winter coat to prepare for the warmer weather, while in fall, they shed lighter summer coats to grow in a thicker, warmer winter coat.

2. **Breed-Specific Shedding Patterns**: Some dog breeds shed more than others. For example, breeds with double coats, such as Huskies, Golden Retrievers, and German Shepherds, tend to shed more because they have an undercoat that helps insulate them from extreme temperatures. These dogs naturally go through seasonal shedding cycles, shedding large amounts of fur.
3. **Health Factors**: A dog's overall health can affect its shedding patterns. Dogs with poor nutrition, hormonal imbalances, stress, or medical conditions may experience excessive shedding. Additionally, dogs going through a life change, like pregnancy or a change in environment, may shed more.
4. **Environmental Factors**: The environment in which your dog lives also plays a significant role in shedding. For instance, dogs living in areas with dry or hot climates might shed more frequently to regulate their body temperature. In contrast, dogs living in colder climates may shed less frequently but still experience seasonal shedding.

Signs of Abnormal Shedding

While shedding is natural, excessive shedding can sometimes be a sign of an underlying health issue. Here are some signs that your dog's shedding may be abnormal:

- Patches of bald spots
- Red, inflamed, or itchy skin
- Increased hair loss that doesn't correlate with the seasons
- Changes in the texture or quality of the fur
- Dull coat appearance, which may suggest poor nutrition or health issues

If you notice any of these signs, it's essential to consult a veterinarian to rule out possible health problems such as allergies, infections, or hormonal imbalances.

Managing Shedding Through Grooming

One of the most effective ways to manage shedding is through regular grooming. Grooming not only helps remove loose hair but also stimulates healthy skin and coat growth. By brushing your dog regularly, you can minimize the amount of hair that ends up on your furniture, clothing, and floors. Grooming also helps maintain a healthy coat, reducing the likelihood of matting, tangles, and discomfort.

Brushing Techniques

1. **Choosing the Right Brush**: The type of brush you use will depend on your dog's coat type. For dogs with short coats, a bristle brush or a rubber brush may suffice. For dogs with long coats or thick undercoats, you may need a slicker brush or a de-shedding tool designed for double coats. Breeds with thick, curly, or wavy hair (like Poodles or Cocker Spaniels) may also benefit from combs that help detangle the fur.
2. **Brushing Frequency**: How often you brush your dog will depend on their breed, coat type, and the amount of shedding. Dogs with short coats, like Beagles and Boxers, may only need to be brushed once a week, while dogs with long or double coats, such as Collies, Golden Retrievers, or Huskies, should be brushed at least two to three times a week, and more during peak shedding seasons.
3. **De-shedding Tools**: If your dog sheds heavily, using a de-shedding tool can help remove excess fur before it falls out.

These tools work by reaching deep into the undercoat to loosen hair without damaging the topcoat. Brands like Furminator and ShedMonster have designed tools specifically for heavy shedders.

4. **Bathing and Brushing**: Regular bathing can also help control shedding by loosening dead hair and making it easier to brush out. Use a dog-friendly shampoo that helps with shedding or a de-shedding conditioner to help reduce the amount of hair lost during brushing.

Managing Dander in Dogs

Dander is another issue that often accompanies shedding. Dander consists of tiny, microscopic flakes of skin shed by your dog, and it can be a significant allergen. While there's no way to completely eliminate dander, there are steps you can take to reduce it and make your home more comfortable for everyone, especially those with allergies.

What is Dander and Why Does It Affect Allergies?

Dander is composed of tiny particles of skin shed by animals, including dogs. These particles can easily become airborne and settle on furniture, carpets, clothing, and other surfaces. When inhaled, dander can trigger allergic reactions, causing symptoms like sneezing, itching, runny nose, and watery eyes in sensitive individuals.

Unlike pet hair, which is larger and more noticeable, dander is microscopic and can linger in the environment even after cleaning. The presence of dander is often the primary cause of allergic reactions, not the fur itself.

Tips for Reducing Dander in Your Home

1. **Frequent Cleaning**: Regular cleaning is essential for reducing dander in your home. Vacuum with a vacuum cleaner equipped with a HEPA filter, which can trap small particles, including dander. Mop floors regularly to prevent dander from settling. Wash your dog's bedding, toys, and any other items they frequently come into contact with to remove accumulated dander.
2. **Air Purifiers**: Air purifiers with HEPA filters can help remove dander from the air. Place an air purifier in rooms where your dog spends the most time or in common areas of your home to reduce allergens and keep the air cleaner.
3. **Wash Your Hands and Clothes**: After handling or grooming your dog, wash your hands thoroughly to avoid transferring dander to other parts of your home. Change your clothes if necessary, especially if you've been in close contact with your dog.
4. **Keep Your Dog Out of Certain Rooms**: If someone in your household has allergies, it's a good idea to keep your dog out of bedrooms or other areas where allergens can accumulate. This will help reduce the buildup of dander in those spaces.
5. **Bathing Your Dog**: Regular bathing can help reduce the amount of dander your dog sheds, as it helps to wash away loose skin flakes. Use a gentle, hypoallergenic dog shampoo designed to minimize dander buildup.
6. **Use Dander-Control Products**: There are several commercial products available that claim to help reduce dander. These include wipes, sprays, and shampoos designed to help control shedding and minimize dander. Although these products may help to some extent, they

should be used in conjunction with other cleaning and grooming methods.

Diet and Health: Impact on Shedding and Dander

Your dog's diet plays a crucial role in the health of their skin and coat. Dogs with poor nutrition may experience excessive shedding and dry, flaky skin, which can contribute to dander production. Ensuring your dog receives a balanced diet rich in essential fatty acids, vitamins, and minerals can improve the overall health of their coat and skin, helping to reduce shedding and dander.

Supplements to Reduce Shedding and Dander

1. **Omega-3 Fatty Acids**: Omega-3s found in fish oils are essential for promoting healthy skin and a shiny coat. Adding an omega-3 supplement to your dog's diet can reduce shedding by improving skin hydration and coat health.
2. **Vitamin E**: This vitamin is vital for skin health and can help reduce dryness, which often leads to excessive shedding and dander.
3. **Probiotics**: Gut health plays a significant role in your dog's skin and coat. Probiotics can help improve digestive health, which, in turn, can enhance the overall health of their skin, reducing excessive shedding and dander production.

While it may not be possible to completely eliminate shedding and dander, you can significantly reduce their impact on your home and your dog's health by following the strategies outlined above.

Chapter 3: Coat Care Techniques

Taking care of your dog's coat is essential not only for maintaining a shiny, healthy appearance but also for ensuring your dog's overall well-being. A well-maintained coat reflects a dog's good health, as it indicates proper grooming, hygiene, and attention to any skin issues.

Coat care techniques vary depending on the type of coat your dog has, and understanding these differences is key to providing the best care.

Whether your dog has a sleek, short coat or a long, flowing mane, regular maintenance is crucial to prevent mats, tangles, and skin irritations. Brushing, trimming, and even specific care routines can help you maintain a beautiful and healthy coat. Additionally, paying attention to any changes in the coat or skin can help detect early signs of underlying health issues like allergies or infections.

This chapter will cover the fundamental coat care techniques, including brushing, trimming, de-shedding, and specific care for different coat types.

With the right tools and knowledge, you'll be equipped to keep your dog's coat in its best condition, ensuring that it's both functional and fabulous. Let's dive into the essential techniques that every dog owner should know to provide the highest level of coat care for their furry companions.

Brushing for Different Coat Types

Brushing your dog's coat is one of the most important aspects of regular grooming, not only to maintain its appearance but also to ensure the health of the skin beneath. Proper brushing removes dirt, debris, and loose hair, stimulates the skin, and promotes healthy hair growth. However, not all dog coats are the same, and different coat types require specific brushing techniques to achieve the best results. Understanding the unique characteristics of your dog's coat type and selecting the right tools and methods will allow you to brush effectively and comfortably.

Short Coat Breeds

Dogs with short coats tend to shed more than long-haired dogs, but their grooming needs are relatively straightforward. Short coats, often seen in breeds like Beagles, Boxers, and Dachsunds, don't mat or tangle like longer coats, but they do require regular brushing to control shedding and maintain a healthy shine.

Brushing Technique for Short Coats:

- **Frequency**: Brushing short-coated dogs two to three times a week is usually sufficient. During shedding seasons, brushing may need to be increased to daily sessions to remove excess hair before it gets onto your furniture and floors.
- **Brush Selection**: A simple bristle brush, a rubber curry brush, or a shedding tool is perfect for short coats. A bristle brush is effective for removing loose hair and distributing natural oils throughout the coat, helping maintain a healthy sheen. Rubber curry brushes are great for massaging the skin

and loosening dead hair, while shedding tools can catch and remove excess fur.
- **Technique**: Brush in the direction of hair growth using gentle, smooth strokes. Start at the neck and work your way down to the tail. Short-haired dogs generally don't need a lot of effort in brushing, but consistency is key. Focus on areas where hair tends to accumulate, such as behind the ears, under the belly, and at the base of the tail.

Medium Coat Breeds

Medium coats are a bit more demanding than short coats, as they tend to tangle and form mats if not properly cared for. Breeds like Cocker Spaniels, Beagles, and Schnauzers are typical examples of medium-coated dogs. These dogs benefit from regular brushing to keep their coats neat and free from tangles, while also controlling shedding.

Brushing Technique for Medium Coats:

- **Frequency**: Medium-coated dogs should be brushed about three to four times a week, especially during their shedding periods, which can be more frequent in the spring and fall.
- **Brush Selection**: A slicker brush or a pin brush is ideal for medium coats. Slicker brushes have fine, closely spaced wires that can remove tangles and mats, while pin brushes have widely spaced pins that help untangle hair without irritating the skin. De-shedding tools and combs can also help with removing loose fur from the undercoat.
- **Technique**: Start by brushing gently with the pin brush to untangle any knots and mats. Once the coat is tangle-free, switch to a slicker brush to remove dead hair from the

undercoat. Brush in the direction of hair growth, and make sure to get into the coat's layers to prevent matting near the skin. Pay special attention to areas like the legs, ears, and underarms, where mats are more likely to form.
- **Tangle Prevention**: For dogs with longer hair that's prone to tangling, consider brushing smaller sections at a time to avoid pulling and breaking the hair. Regular trimming of the coat also helps to prevent the buildup of mats.

Long Coat Breeds

Long coats are the most high-maintenance type, requiring regular and thorough brushing to prevent mats and tangles, which can lead to discomfort or even skin problems if left untreated. Breeds like Yorkshire Terriers, Shih Tzus, and Collies are known for their long, flowing coats, and they require frequent care to keep their coats looking their best.

Brushing Technique for Long Coats:

- **Frequency**: Long-haired dogs need to be brushed at least four to five times a week, and often daily during periods of shedding. These dogs are prone to tangles and mats, which need to be removed promptly to avoid discomfort or skin irritation.
- **Brush Selection**: A combination of tools is often needed for long coats. Start with a wide-toothed comb or pin brush to gently detangle the hair. Once the coat is smooth, use a slicker brush to remove loose hair and any tangles that may have formed deeper in the coat. For very fine or silky coats, a soft bristle brush may be used for finishing touches to add shine.

- **Technique**: Work in sections to prevent pulling and breakage. Begin at the ends of the coat and slowly work your way toward the roots, gently detangling any knots. If mats are found, use your fingers to gently pull apart the hair or a mat splitter tool to avoid tugging on the hair. Once the coat is fully untangled, use a slicker brush to remove loose undercoat and smooth the top layer. Brushing in layers ensures you're not missing any hair, especially near the skin, where mats are more likely to form.
- **Additional Tips for Long Coats**: Long-haired dogs require regular baths and conditionings to prevent their coats from becoming dry and prone to tangling. Regular trimming or "maintenance cuts" are also advisable, especially around the paws, ears, and tail, where hair tends to mat more quickly.

Double Coat Breeds

Double coats are made up of two layers: a dense undercoat and a longer, coarser outer coat. These coats are commonly seen in breeds like Huskies, Golden Retrievers, and German Shepherds. Double-coated dogs shed heavily, especially during the spring and fall when they "blow" their coat to prepare for changing weather. Managing a double coat requires specific techniques to remove excess hair and maintain the health of both the undercoat and the outer layer.

Brushing Technique for Double Coats:

- **Frequency**: Double-coated dogs typically require brushing three to four times a week, with more frequent sessions during heavy shedding periods. During their coat "blow" phase, you may need to brush daily to prevent mats and reduce shedding indoors.

- **Brush Selection**: A de-shedding tool is a must-have for double-coated dogs. The Furminator is a popular choice, as it removes loose undercoat hair without damaging the outer coat. Additionally, a slicker brush can be used for general brushing and to remove tangles, while a pin brush can help separate the undercoat from the topcoat.
- **Technique**: Start by using a de-shedding tool to gently work through the undercoat, removing loose hair. This can be a time-consuming process, as double-coated dogs often shed large amounts of fur. After de-shedding, use a slicker brush to work through the topcoat, removing any tangles or mats. Be sure to brush the coat in layers, working from the skin outward to ensure that you're reaching the undercoat. Pay particular attention to areas like behind the ears, under the legs, and at the base of the tail, where mats tend to form.

Curly and Wavy Coat Breeds

Curly and wavy coats, commonly seen in breeds like Poodles, Bichon Frises, and Cockapoos, require consistent care to maintain their texture and prevent matting. These coats can easily become tangled if not brushed regularly, as the curly or wavy texture can trap loose hair and dirt.

Brushing Technique for Curly and Wavy Coats:

- **Frequency**: Dogs with curly or wavy coats need to be brushed at least three to four times a week, but often more frequently if they have long hair. Matting can occur quickly in curly coats, so regular attention is essential.
- **Brush Selection**: A pin brush or wide-toothed comb works well to detangle curly and wavy coats. A slicker brush can

help remove dead hair and prevent mats, while a de-matting comb can be useful for more severe tangles.
- **Technique**: Begin by using a wide-toothed comb to gently detangle the coat, starting from the ends and working upward toward the roots. For any knots or mats, work slowly with your fingers or a specialized de-matting comb to avoid pulling the hair. Once the coat is detangled, use a slicker brush to smooth it out and remove any remaining loose hair. Pay particular attention to the underarms, behind the ears, and around the legs, where mats are more likely to develop.
- **Additional Care**: Regular trimming helps to keep curly coats manageable and reduce the likelihood of mats forming. Be sure to visit a groomer for professional trims if your dog's coat becomes too difficult to manage on your own.

Each dog's coat is unique, and understanding how to properly brush your dog based on its coat type will lead to healthier skin and a shinier, more beautiful coat. Remember, consistent grooming is not only about appearance—it's about maintaining your dog's health, comfort, and happiness. Keep brushing sessions positive and calm, making them a bonding experience between you and your dog while taking care of their grooming needs.

Trimming and Styling Essentials

Trimming and styling are key components of dog grooming, ensuring that your dog's coat remains tidy, healthy, and in top condition. While regular brushing helps to remove tangles, mats, and loose hair, trimming and styling serve to keep the coat at a manageable length, enhance the dog's appearance, and address any specific needs based on the breed, coat type, or health considerations. Whether you're looking to simply trim a few stray hairs or give your dog a full makeover, understanding the essential tools, techniques, and best practices for trimming and styling is crucial.

Proper trimming and styling are not only about aesthetics—they also contribute to your dog's overall comfort. Overgrown or unruly hair can lead to mats, skin irritation, and difficulty moving, particularly in areas like the paws, ears, and around the eyes. This section will guide you through the essential trimming and styling techniques for different coat types, the tools you'll need, and helpful tips to ensure a safe, effective grooming experience.

Understanding the Need for Trimming and Styling

Trimming is not just about keeping your dog looking neat—it also serves several functional purposes:

- **Health and Comfort**: Long or overgrown hair can hinder your dog's mobility, cause discomfort, and even contribute to skin issues like hot spots or fungal infections. Regular trimming can alleviate these concerns by keeping hair at a manageable length.
- **Aesthetic Appeal**: Certain breeds are traditionally groomed in specific styles to reflect the breed's characteristics, such as the Poodle's signature cut or the Shih Tzu's luxurious long coat. Regular styling helps your dog look its best and maintains the breed's appearance.
- **Maintenance**: Some dog breeds, particularly those with long or thick coats, benefit from trimming to prevent matting. Trimming also helps maintain the coat's overall health by reducing tangles and preventing debris from becoming trapped in the fur.

While trimming can be done at home, certain styles may require professional grooming expertise. However, even if you opt for a groomer, learning basic trimming skills can help you maintain your dog's coat between grooming visits.

The Right Tools for Trimming and Styling

Before diving into the techniques for trimming and styling, it's essential to have the right tools for the job. Here's a rundown of the most common tools used in dog trimming and styling:

- **Clippers**: Dog clippers are specially designed for trimming dog hair and are equipped with a variety of blades for different coat types. Clippers come in corded or cordless models, and each has its own power levels and features to accommodate different needs. When choosing a clipper, ensure it's suited to the thickness of your dog's coat. For example, heavier, thicker coats will require clippers with more power and wider blades.
- **Scissors**: Scissors are necessary for finer detail work, such as trimming around the eyes, ears, paws, and tail. Straight scissors are used for general trimming, while curved scissors are great for shaping the coat around tricky areas. Thinning shears can also be useful for reducing volume in thick coats without cutting the hair too short.
- **Combs**: Combs are essential for detangling hair and parting the coat before cutting. A wide-toothed comb is ideal for thick or matted coats, while a finer-toothed comb works well for shorter or finer hair.
- **Nail Clippers**: While primarily used for trimming nails, nail clippers can also be used for trimming the hair around the paws. Regular nail trimming is an important part of

grooming, as overgrown nails can lead to discomfort and affect your dog's gait.
- **Grooming Brushes**: Brushes help to untangle mats and distribute natural oils throughout the coat, ensuring that the hair is in the best condition before trimming. A slicker brush or a pin brush is often used before clipping to remove tangles and ensure the coat is smooth.
- **Grooming Table**: A sturdy grooming table with a non-slip surface can make the trimming process more comfortable and efficient for both you and your dog. Many tables come with adjustable heights, which allows you to work at an ergonomic level.

By investing in high-quality tools and regularly maintaining them, you ensure that your dog's grooming process is efficient and safe.

Trimming Techniques for Different Coat Types

The trimming techniques for different dog coat types vary depending on the texture, length, and grooming needs of the breed. Let's take a look at how to approach trimming for various coat types:

Short Coat Dogs
Short coat dogs, such as Bulldogs, Beagles, and Dachshunds, generally require less frequent trimming. However, there are still areas that benefit from occasional touch-ups, particularly around the paws, face, and tail.

Trimming Technique:

- **General Trimming**: For short coats, the main focus is on maintaining the dog's natural shape. Use clippers with a #10

or #15 blade for general trimming, particularly around the neck, belly, and legs.
- **Paw and Face Care**: Use scissors to carefully trim the fur around the paws and face to keep these areas tidy and free from irritation. Be cautious when trimming the face, especially around the eyes, to avoid nicks.
- **Tail**: The tail area may require trimming to maintain a natural, balanced look. Use clippers with a shorter guard or scissors for finer detailing.

Medium Coat Dogs

Medium coat breeds, such as Cocker Spaniels, Border Collies, and Australian Shepherds, require more attention in terms of trimming to prevent tangles and matting, particularly in areas with longer fur like the ears, underbelly, and legs.

Trimming Technique:

- **Tidy Up the Body**: Use clippers to trim the body, maintaining a natural look while preventing hair from becoming too long and tangled. A #4 or #5 blade will often provide a nice length.
- **Legs and Belly**: Medium coats can quickly tangle on the legs and underbelly, so regular trimming is necessary. Use scissors to trim excess hair, ensuring a smooth transition from the body to the legs.
- **Facial Grooming**: Trim around the eyes, ears, and mouth to keep the face clean and neat. Use curved scissors for precision and to avoid injury.

Long Coat Dogs

Long-haired dogs, like Yorkshire Terriers, Shih Tzus, and Lhasa

Apsos, require regular trimming to maintain their stunning appearance and avoid matting. Long coats can become matted quickly, especially around the ears, neck, and belly, making it important to trim and shape the hair regularly.

Trimming Technique:

- **Trim to Maintain Length**: Use clippers with a longer blade or scissors to maintain the dog's desired coat length. Be cautious around sensitive areas like the face and ears to avoid accidental cuts.
- **Shaping the Coat**: For dogs with long, flowing hair, the aim is often to enhance their natural shape. Begin by trimming the body, leaving the legs and tail to flow naturally. Use scissors to blend the top coat into the undercoat, especially around the neck and chest.
- **Face and Ears**: Long-haired dogs often benefit from a trim around the face and ears to prevent hair from obstructing vision and causing irritation. Use curved scissors to carefully shape the hair around the eyes, nose, and mouth.

Double-Coat Dogs

Double-coated dogs, like Huskies, Golden Retrievers, and German Shepherds, need regular grooming to prevent mats and to manage the heavy shedding they experience. Trimming is not usually necessary for the coat itself, but regular maintenance ensures that the coat stays healthy and manageable.

Trimming Technique:

- **De-shedding**: Use a de-shedding tool or undercoat rake to remove loose hair from the undercoat. This reduces the shedding in your home and prevents mats from forming.
- **Edge Trimming**: Trim around the paws, tail, and ears using scissors to maintain a neat and balanced look. Be careful not to trim the dense undercoat, as it serves to regulate body temperature.
- **Avoid Over-Trimming**: It's essential not to cut the topcoat too short, as it protects your dog from the sun and elements. Stick to trimming the edges and any areas that naturally become matted or dirty.

Curly and Wavy Coat Dogs

Curly and wavy-coated dogs, such as Poodles, Bichon Frises, and Cockapoos, require frequent trimming to keep their coats in shape. The hair can become tangled and matted quickly, so regular visits to the groomer or careful at-home maintenance is necessary.

Trimming Technique:

- **Regular Shaping**: For curly and wavy coats, trimming should focus on maintaining the natural shape of the coat while removing tangles and mats. Use clippers to trim the body to the desired length, and scissors to refine the face, ears, and paws.
- **Curved Scissors for Detail**: Curved scissors are essential for trimming around the face, ears, and tail, where precision is required to avoid cutting too much or too little.
- **Thinning Shears for Volume**: Use thinning shears to reduce the volume of a thick coat, particularly in areas like the chest or neck, where the coat can become dense and difficult to manage.

Trimming and styling your dog's coat can be an enjoyable and rewarding experience, ensuring your dog looks great and feels comfortable. If you're ever unsure about how to achieve a specific style, consulting with a professional groomer can help you learn more advanced techniques and maintain your dog's appearance at its best.

Dealing with Mats, Tangles, and Knots

Mats, tangles, and knots are common challenges faced by dog owners, especially those with dogs who have long, curly, or thick coats. These hair issues can be not only unsightly but also uncomfortable or even painful for your dog if left unaddressed. The buildup of mats and tangles can trap dirt, moisture, and even parasites against your dog's skin, potentially leading to skin irritation, infections, or hot spots. For some dogs, these issues can result in hair loss or damage to the coat. Understanding how to prevent, identify, and remove mats and tangles is essential for keeping your dog's coat in top condition and ensuring their comfort and well-being.

In this section, we will explore the causes of mats and tangles, how to prevent them, and step-by-step techniques for safely and effectively removing them. Whether you are a seasoned dog owner or new to grooming, these tips will help you handle any matting or tangling situation and keep your dog's coat looking healthy, shiny, and smooth.

Causes of Mats and Tangles

Mats and tangles develop when the hair becomes intertwined or twisted, creating clumps that are difficult to remove. Several factors contribute to the formation of mats and tangles:

- **Coat Type**: Certain dog coat types are more prone to matting than others. Long-haired dogs, curly-coated breeds, and double-coated dogs are especially vulnerable to mats and tangles. For example, breeds like Poodles, Shih Tzus, and Cocker Spaniels have coats that can easily tangle without regular grooming.
- **Lack of Regular Grooming**: Mats and tangles form when dead hair, dirt, and debris are not removed regularly through brushing. Without frequent brushing, the natural oils in the coat, combined with dirt and loose hair, can lead to mats and tangles, especially in areas where hair tends to rub together or collect moisture, such as behind the ears, around the collar area, and under the legs.
- **Moisture and Humidity**: Wet hair is more prone to tangling. Dogs who get wet frequently, whether from rain, swimming, or bathing, are more susceptible to mats forming if their coat is not dried properly. Even humid weather can cause the hair to stick together and create tangles.
- **Friction**: Areas of the dog's body that experience frequent movement or friction can develop mats faster. Common problem spots include the area behind the ears, the armpits, the groin area, and the base of the tail, where the hair tends to rub against the body and cause knots to form.
- **Health Issues**: In some cases, mats and tangles may indicate an underlying health issue, such as obesity, mobility problems, or skin conditions. For example, a dog with arthritis or hip dysplasia may not be able to groom itself effectively, leading to mats forming in areas it cannot reach.

Additionally, dogs suffering from allergies or skin infections may have patches of hair that clump together due to irritation.

Preventing Mats, Tangles, and Knots

Prevention is always better than dealing with mats and tangles once they have formed. Regular grooming is essential for maintaining a mat-free coat and preventing hair problems before they arise. Here are some tips for preventing mats and tangles:

- **Regular Brushing**: Brushing your dog regularly, at least once or twice a week for most breeds, helps to remove dead hair, dirt, and debris that can contribute to matting. For dogs with long, thick, or curly coats, daily brushing may be necessary to keep mats from forming. Make sure to use the appropriate brush for your dog's coat type.
- **Use the Right Tools**: The tools you use to groom your dog can make a huge difference in preventing mats. A slicker brush, pin brush, or undercoat rake is ideal for detangling and preventing mats in long-haired or double-coated dogs. For curly coats, use a comb or de-matting rake to gently work through tangles and prevent the hair from getting too knotted.
- **Avoid Over-Bathing**: Bathing your dog too frequently can strip its coat of natural oils, leading to dry, brittle hair that is more likely to tangle. Bathing should be done only when necessary, and always use a high-quality dog shampoo and conditioner to help maintain the health and moisture balance of the coat.
- **Drying Properly After Baths**: If your dog has been in the water, make sure to dry their coat thoroughly after bathing

or swimming. Wet hair is more prone to tangling, so it's important to gently towel-dry your dog and then use a blow dryer on a low, cool setting to dry the coat fully. If your dog has a particularly thick or long coat, you may want to consider using a professional grooming dryer.
- **Regular Trimming**: Keeping the hair at a manageable length is key to preventing mats and tangles. Dogs with longer coats often benefit from regular trimming to prevent hair from becoming too long and difficult to manage. Some dogs may need to be trimmed every few weeks, while others may only require a trim a few times a year.
- **Check Problem Areas**: Be extra diligent in checking areas of your dog's coat that are more prone to mats and tangles, such as under the ears, behind the legs, around the neck, and the belly. These areas often experience friction or are more likely to collect moisture, making them prone to tangling. Regularly check these spots and remove any tangles or mats as soon as they appear.

How to Remove Mats, Tangles, and Knots

Despite best efforts, mats and tangles can still form, especially in dogs with long or dense coats. When this happens, it's important to address the issue promptly to prevent it from worsening and causing discomfort for your dog. Here's how to safely and effectively remove mats and tangles:

Detangling Before Cutting
When faced with a tangle or mat, it's important to avoid rushing into cutting or shaving the area. Instead, begin by gently working through the mat using a detangling comb or brush. Start from the ends of the hair and work your way up to the base of the mat, being

gentle to avoid pulling on the hair or causing pain to your dog. Be patient and take breaks if needed, as the process can be time-consuming, especially with thick mats.

Use a Mat Remover or Dematting Tool
For more stubborn mats, a dematting rake or mat remover can be helpful. These tools are specifically designed to tackle dense mats without causing harm to the skin. Work the tool gently through the mat in a back-and-forth motion, starting from the outer edge and moving toward the skin. Avoid using excessive force, as this can cause discomfort or injury.

Break the Mat with Your Fingers
If the mat is relatively small or located in an easily accessible area, you can sometimes use your fingers to gently break it apart before brushing it out. Gently separate the hair using your fingers, loosening the strands before combing through with a brush or comb.

Cutting Mats and Tangles
In some cases, mats may be too tight or too close to the skin to remove with brushing alone. If this happens, you may need to trim or cut the mat out. Always use scissors that are specifically designed for dog grooming to avoid injury. Carefully cut around the mat, making sure not to cut too close to the skin. If you're unsure about cutting a mat, it's always safer to seek the help of a professional groomer to avoid causing harm to your dog.

Prevent Future Mats with Regular Grooming
Once the mats and tangles have been removed, it's essential to continue regular grooming to prevent future issues. Brushing daily or weekly, depending on your dog's coat type, and ensuring proper care will help maintain a smooth, tangle-free coat.

Working with Sensitive Areas

Certain areas of your dog's body are more sensitive than others, making them more prone to discomfort or injury when mats or tangles occur. Here's how to approach grooming sensitive spots with care:

- **Around the Eyes**: Tangles around the eyes are common in many breeds, especially those with long, flowing hair. Use a fine-toothed comb or curved scissors to carefully trim the hair around the eyes. Avoid pulling or tugging at tangles, as the skin around the eyes is delicate.
- **Behind the Ears**: Mats often form behind the ears, where moisture, sweat, and dirt accumulate. Use a pin brush to gently detangle the hair around the ears and avoid pulling on the skin. If mats are present, carefully work them out with a detangling tool before trimming any excess hair.
- **Under the Legs and Belly**: The belly and the areas under the legs are also prone to matting. Work gently through any tangles in these areas and use thinning shears if necessary to trim the hair for better hygiene and comfort.

When to Seek Professional Help

If you encounter severe matting, or if your dog is particularly anxious or resistant to grooming, it may be best to seek professional grooming help. Groomers are trained to handle complex mats, especially in sensitive or hard-to-reach areas, and they have the right tools and experience to ensure the process is safe and comfortable for your dog. Regular visits to a professional groomer can also help maintain your dog's coat and prevent mats from becoming a recurring issue.

Mats, tangles, and knots are a common concern for many dog owners, particularly those with long-haired or curly-coated breeds. If mats do form, it's essential to handle them with care, using the proper techniques to remove them safely. Regular grooming is key to maintaining a healthy, comfortable coat for your dog, ensuring they look and feel their best.

Seasonal Grooming Tips

Grooming your dog is an essential aspect of maintaining their health and well-being, but the grooming needs of your dog can change with the seasons. From the heat of summer to the chill of winter, seasonal changes can impact your dog's coat, skin, and general hygiene. Understanding how the environment affects your dog's grooming needs is crucial for keeping their coat in top condition throughout the year. Seasonal grooming isn't just about making your dog look great; it also helps prevent skin problems, discomfort, and health issues that can arise from changes in weather.

In this section, we will explore essential seasonal grooming tips that will ensure your dog remains comfortable, healthy, and well-groomed year-round. Whether you're preparing for the cold weather months or the heat of summer, these tips will help you navigate the unique challenges of each season and ensure your dog is well taken care of.

Spring Grooming Tips

As the weather warms up in the spring, your dog's grooming needs may change. The shedding season begins, especially for dogs with double coats, and allergens from the environment may affect your dog's skin and coat. Spring grooming also includes preparations for summer, so it's important to start early.

Prepare for Shedding Season

Spring is when many dogs start to shed their winter coats. Double-coated dogs like Huskies, Golden Retrievers, and German Shepherds shed heavily during this time. Frequent brushing during this season is crucial to prevent mats and tangles from forming, which can trap excess hair and cause discomfort. Brushing daily or at least a few times a week will help remove loose fur and prevent hair from accumulating in the house.

- **Use an Undercoat Rake**: For dogs with thick undercoats, use an undercoat rake or de-shedding tool to remove the excess undercoat. This will help reduce shedding and make your dog's coat lighter for the warmer months.
- **Bathing**: Giving your dog a bath during spring can help remove excess fur and dander. Use a mild, dog-friendly shampoo to cleanse the coat and help reduce allergens. Make sure to thoroughly dry the coat after the bath, as moisture can contribute to tangling and matting.
- **Allergy Protection**: Spring is allergy season, and many dogs experience skin irritation, itching, or redness due to pollen and other environmental allergens. Be sure to bathe your dog regularly, using hypoallergenic shampoos, and keep their living environment clean to reduce allergens. You can also wipe down their paws and coat with a damp cloth after walks to minimize pollen exposure.

Trim Nails and Hair Around Sensitive Areas

As the weather warms up, your dog may become more active, which means the need for nail trimming increases. Long nails can cause discomfort and can even lead to injury. Trim your dog's nails regularly, especially if they're active outdoors. You should also keep the hair around their paws trimmed to avoid dirt and debris from accumulating in the fur, which can irritate the skin.

Spring is a great time to trim the hair around sensitive areas such as the eyes, ears, and rear end. This helps prevent the accumulation of dirt, bacteria, and mats in those spots.

Summer Grooming Tips

Hot weather can be uncomfortable and even dangerous for some dogs, particularly those with long, dense, or double coats. Proper grooming during the summer can help prevent overheating, reduce the risk of skin conditions, and keep your dog comfortable in the heat.

Keep Your Dog Cool and Comfortable

In hot weather, it's essential to groom your dog in a way that helps them stay cool. One of the most important grooming tasks is to keep your dog's coat well-maintained.

- **Clipping and Trimming**: If you have a long-haired dog, consider giving them a trim or a summer cut to reduce the amount of hair that can trap heat. However, avoid shaving the coat entirely, as it provides important protection from the sun. For double-coated breeds, it's important to maintain the undercoat to prevent sunburn on the skin.

- **Frequent Baths**: Summer heat and humidity can lead to dirt, dust, and sweat building up in your dog's coat. Regular baths will keep your dog feeling fresh and help maintain skin health. Be sure to use a gentle, moisturizing shampoo to keep their skin from drying out. After bathing, thoroughly dry your dog's coat with a towel or blow dryer set to cool or low heat to avoid moisture buildup, which can lead to infections or matting.

Protect Against Fleas and Ticks

Summer is prime flea and tick season, and these pests can cause significant discomfort and even serious health problems for your dog. Regular grooming during the summer months helps detect fleas, ticks, and other external parasites early. Check your dog's coat thoroughly for signs of fleas, ticks, or other pests.

- **Use Flea and Tick Treatments**: Along with grooming, ensure that you use proper flea and tick preventative treatments. Consult your vet about the best options for your dog, whether they're topical treatments, oral medications, or collars.
- **Bathing for Pest Control**: Special flea shampoos can help get rid of fleas and ticks if your dog has been exposed to them. Regular bathing with these shampoos can help control infestations.

Protecting from Sunburn

Dogs with thin or light-colored coats are especially susceptible to sunburn. Areas like the ears, nose, and belly can burn quickly if exposed to direct sunlight for extended periods. You can protect your dog from sunburn by applying dog-safe sunscreen to these areas before outdoor activities or using protective clothing like UV-resistant shirts or bandanas. Long-haired dogs should be kept in the shade and avoid direct sun exposure when possible.

Fall Grooming Tips

As the temperatures begin to drop in the fall, your dog may start growing a thicker coat in preparation for the winter months. Fall is also a time when shedding may increase again, and your dog's grooming needs may shift accordingly.

Maintain Regular Brushing

In the fall, shedding from the summer heat typically slows down, but this is when your dog starts growing its thicker winter coat. Double-coated breeds, such as Collies, Bernese Mountain Dogs, and Newfoundlands, may begin to shed heavily during this transitional period. Regular brushing helps remove dead hair and loose fur, keeping your dog's coat in top condition as it adjusts to the cooler weather.

- **Use the Right Brushes**: Bristle brushes and slicker brushes are great for managing your dog's coat during this transition. If you have a double-coated dog, using an undercoat rake or comb can help remove dead undercoat and reduce shedding.

Prepare for Winter

As the weather gets colder, it's important to make preparations for winter grooming. Dogs with thicker coats may need to be trimmed less often, but it's essential to make sure their coats are properly maintained to keep them warm and comfortable.

- **Trim Hair Around the Paws and Ears**: Fall is a great time to trim excess hair around your dog's paws and ears. This helps to keep your dog from collecting leaves, snow, or ice in these areas, which can cause discomfort or even injury. Trimming hair around the paws also prevents the buildup of dirt and debris that can irritate the skin.

Winter Grooming Tips

Winter weather can present its own set of grooming challenges. Cold temperatures, wet conditions, and salt or chemicals on the ground can all affect your dog's coat and skin. Ensuring that your dog is properly groomed for winter can help keep them comfortable and healthy.

Prevent Dry Skin and Coat Damage

Cold, dry air in winter can lead to dry, flaky skin in dogs, especially those who are already prone to skin issues. Bathing your dog too often during winter can strip away natural oils, leading to dry skin and irritation. It's important to bathe your dog only as necessary and use moisturizing shampoos designed for dry skin.

- **Moisturizing Shampoos**: Opt for shampoos and conditioners with moisturizing properties to help hydrate your dog's skin and coat during the dry winter months. Avoid human shampoos, as they can be too harsh on your dog's skin.

- **Use Leave-In Conditioners**: Leave-in conditioners can help keep your dog's coat soft and hydrated during the winter months. These conditioners are designed to provide extra moisture and prevent dryness.

Dry and Clean After Outdoor Play

After outdoor walks or playtime in the snow, it's important to dry off your dog thoroughly. Snow and ice can collect in your dog's paws, causing discomfort and potential skin irritation. Drying your dog's paws and coat with a towel will help prevent ice buildup and reduce the chances of your dog developing skin issues.

- **Paw Care**: Salt and chemicals used to melt snow on roads and sidewalks can irritate your dog's paws. After each walk, wipe your dog's paws with a damp cloth to remove any harmful substances and prevent them from licking them off. You can also apply a protective paw balm to keep your dog's paw pads soft and free from cracks.

Seasonal grooming is an important part of keeping your dog healthy and comfortable year-round. Whether it's preparing for the summer heat, dealing with shedding in the spring, or taking extra precautions during the winter months, understanding your dog's grooming needs throughout the seasons can make a big difference in their well-being.

Chapter 4: Nail, Paw, and Skin Care

Taking care of your dog's nails, paws, and skin is a vital part of their overall grooming routine. These areas often go unnoticed, but they play a crucial role in your dog's comfort and health.

Regular attention to your dog's nails, paws, and skin helps prevent discomfort, injury, and infections, ensuring that your dog stays active and happy.

In this chapter, we will explore the importance of maintaining your dog's nails, paws, and skin. From understanding when and how to trim nails to keeping paws clean and moisturized, we'll cover essential techniques and products that support your dog's well-being.

Additionally, skin care will be discussed in detail, as a healthy coat and skin contribute to overall health and comfort, preventing dryness, irritation, and infections.

Whether your dog enjoys outdoor adventures, daily walks, or lounging at home, their nails, paws, and skin require consistent care to stay in top shape.

This chapter will guide you through the best practices for maintaining these areas, highlighting preventive measures and practical tips to keep your dog feeling their best year-round. Through proper care, you'll ensure that your dog's paws remain soft, their nails stay healthy, and their skin is free from irritation or discomfort.

Nail Trimming: Tools and Techniques

Nail trimming is an essential part of your dog's grooming routine. While it may seem like a small task, keeping your dog's nails properly trimmed is vital to their overall health and comfort. Overgrown nails can cause discomfort, lead to potential injury, and even result in postural problems or difficulty walking. Nail trimming, when done correctly, can help prevent these issues and maintain your dog's well-being.

In this section, we will explore everything you need to know about nail trimming for your dog, including the best tools for the job, proper techniques, and tips to ensure a safe and effective nail care routine.

Understanding Why Nail Trimming Is Important

Regular nail trimming helps ensure that your dog's nails don't grow too long, which can lead to various health issues. Long nails can cause your dog to walk awkwardly, potentially leading to joint and bone strain. Additionally, overly long nails can catch on surfaces or become cracked or split, leading to painful injuries or infections. By trimming your dog's nails regularly, you'll help avoid these problems and keep your dog moving comfortably.

Nail trimming also ensures that the quick (the sensitive tissue inside the nail that contains blood vessels and nerves) does not grow too long. If the quick is allowed to grow with the nail, it will become exposed during trimming, leading to bleeding and pain. Regular trimming helps keep the quick short, making each trimming easier and more comfortable for your dog.

Tools for Nail Trimming

The right tools are crucial for a successful nail trimming session. Various nail trimming tools are available, and choosing the right one for your dog's size and temperament is essential for both safety and effectiveness.

Nail Clippers

Nail clippers are the most common tool for trimming dog nails. There are different types of clippers designed to fit various dog sizes and nail thicknesses. Understanding which clipper to use can make the job easier and ensure a clean cut.

- **Scissor-Type Clippers**: These clippers resemble a pair of scissors, with two sharp blades that come together to cut the nail. They are ideal for small to medium-sized dogs and offer good control for precision trimming. Scissor-type clippers are often favored for their ergonomic design, making them comfortable for the groomer to use.
- **Guillotine-Type Clippers**: These clippers have a small hole where the nail is placed. When you squeeze the handles, a blade inside the hole cuts the nail. Guillotine-type clippers are commonly used for dogs with smaller nails, and they are simple to use. However, they may not be the best option for larger dogs or those with very thick nails.
- **Plier-Type Clippers**: Plier-type clippers resemble pliers and have a spring-loaded mechanism. These clippers are ideal for larger dogs or dogs with thick nails, as they provide more force and can cut through tougher nails. They are

especially useful for dogs with hard, tough nails, such as large breeds or working dogs.

When choosing a nail clipper, make sure it's the right size for your dog. Clippers that are too large or too small can be difficult to handle and may lead to uneven cuts or injury.

Nail Grinder

While clippers are effective for trimming nails, a nail grinder offers a different approach by gradually grinding down the nail. This tool is typically powered by electricity or batteries and uses a rotating drum to smooth and shorten the nail. Nail grinders can be particularly useful for dogs with thick nails or those who may be afraid of clippers, as they provide a gentler alternative.

Grinders are ideal for dogs who are nervous about the sound or sensation of nail clippers. They allow for more control over the amount of nail being removed and can be less intimidating for your dog. However, nail grinders tend to take longer than clippers and can be messy, so they may require more patience.

Nail File

A nail file is typically used after the nails have been trimmed to smooth out rough edges and prevent the nails from snagging. Nail files come in various shapes and sizes, and there are specific dog nail files designed to make this task easier. This tool is especially useful for dogs who have particularly brittle or fragile nails that may splinter or crack after clipping. It's also helpful to use a file to round the edges of the nails and prevent painful snags.

Though nail files are not typically used to trim nails themselves, they are essential for finishing up the grooming session and ensuring your dog's nails are smooth and comfortable.

Styptic Powder

Accidents can happen while trimming nails, and sometimes the quick may be accidentally cut, leading to bleeding. Styptic powder is a crucial tool to have on hand during nail trimming. This powder helps stop bleeding quickly and prevents further discomfort. Styptic powder is applied directly to the bleeding nail, and it works by constricting the blood vessels and forming a clot to stop the flow of blood.

In case of an accident, styptic powder is an essential tool to minimize pain and prevent infection.

Proper Techniques for Nail Trimming

Now that you have the right tools, it's time to learn how to trim your dog's nails correctly. Nail trimming can be a delicate process, and if done improperly, it can lead to injury or make your dog anxious about future grooming sessions. Below are step-by-step techniques to ensure a safe and effective nail trimming experience for both you and your dog.

Preparing Your Dog

Before beginning the nail trimming process, it's important to prepare your dog for the session. Dogs can be anxious or fearful about having their nails trimmed, so it's essential to create a calm and positive environment.

- **Introduce the Tools Slowly**: Allow your dog to get used to the sight and sound of the clippers or grinder before you begin. Gently touch your dog's paws with your hands and gradually introduce the tool, so they feel more comfortable with the process.
- **Calm Environment**: Choose a quiet space for grooming where your dog won't be distracted or frightened. A calm environment helps reduce anxiety and makes the process smoother.
- **Positive Reinforcement**: Use treats and praise to reward your dog after each nail is trimmed. This will help create a positive association with the grooming process, making it easier for both you and your dog in the future.

Trimming the Nails

- **Positioning**: Hold your dog's paw firmly but gently. If your dog is nervous, you can wrap them in a towel or have someone else help hold the dog in place. Take your time to ensure your dog is comfortable before beginning the trim.
- **Locate the Quick**: The quick is the pinkish area inside the nail, and it contains blood vessels and nerves. You should avoid cutting into the quick, as it can be painful and cause bleeding. In light-colored nails, you can easily see the quick, but in dark nails, you may need to trim a little at a time until you notice the nail begin to curve downwards.
- **Trimming in Small Increments**: When trimming the nails, cut in small increments to avoid cutting into the quick. Trim a small amount of the nail at a time, working from the tip back toward the base. If you're unsure, it's better to trim less than more to avoid cutting too deep.

- **Use the Right Angle**: Make sure to clip the nails at a slight angle to follow the natural shape of the nail. This will help avoid sharp edges and make the nail more comfortable for your dog.
- **Stay Calm**: It's important to remain calm throughout the trimming process. If your dog is anxious or scared, take breaks and try again later. Rushing through the process can lead to mistakes and create more stress for both you and your dog.

Handling Accidents

If you accidentally cut the quick and your dog's nail starts bleeding, don't panic. Use styptic powder to stop the bleeding. Apply the powder directly to the nail and gently apply pressure. If the bleeding persists, contact your vet for further assistance.

Nail trimming is an essential part of your dog's grooming routine, and with the right tools and techniques, it can be a smooth and stress-free experience for both you and your dog. Regular nail trimming not only prevents injuries and discomfort but also helps your dog move more freely and maintain optimal health. Always remember to keep your dog calm, use positive reinforcement, and take extra care when handling their paws.

Paw Pad Care and Moisturizing

The health of your dog's paws is vital for their overall well-being, as they play a central role in your dog's mobility, comfort, and ability to perform everyday activities. Paw pads are tough, but they can still be prone to issues like dryness, cracks, abrasions, and irritation. Taking care of your dog's paw pads is essential not only for comfort but also for preventing painful conditions that could lead to further health complications. In this section, we will explore the importance of paw pad care, effective moisturizing techniques, and essential tips for ensuring your dog's paws stay healthy and protected.

Understanding the Structure of the Paw Pads

Paw pads are designed to protect the underlying bones and tissues of your dog's feet. These pads are composed of a thick layer of fatty tissue covered by a tough, rough surface of skin. The pads are highly specialized for a variety of purposes, including shock absorption, traction, temperature regulation, and protection from injury. There are typically five pads on each of your dog's paws: the digital pads (located beneath each toe), the metacarpal/metatarsal pad (on the main part of the paw), and the carpal pad (on the back of the front legs).

While paw pads are tough and resilient, they can become dry, cracked, or damaged due to various factors such as weather, rough surfaces, or lack of moisture. Paw pads also require special attention in particular weather conditions, such as the harsh winter cold or intense summer heat. Without proper care, these pads can suffer from pain, cracking, bleeding, or infection, leading to discomfort and decreased mobility for your dog.

Why Paw Pad Care is Essential

Just like your dog's coat, their paws require regular maintenance and attention to stay in optimal condition. Poor paw care can lead to a variety of problems, including:

- **Cracked and Dry Pads**: Dry, cracked paw pads are common during the winter months or after walking on rough, abrasive surfaces. Cracks in the paw pads can be painful for your dog and may even result in infections if not properly treated.
- **Paw Pad Burns**: In hot weather, walking on pavement or other hot surfaces can cause burns to your dog's paw pads. This can lead to painful blisters or peeling skin, which can make walking or running difficult for your dog.
- **Infections**: Paw pads are susceptible to cuts, abrasions, and infections from foreign objects, such as glass, splinters, or dirt. If the pads are not cared for properly, these injuries can worsen and cause infections that are painful and require veterinary attention.
- **Allergic Reactions**: Your dog's paws are exposed to a wide range of environmental allergens, including pollen, dust, and chemicals. If your dog has an allergic reaction, their paws may become irritated, itchy, and inflamed.
- **General Discomfort**: Without proper moisturizing and care, your dog may experience discomfort while walking, running, or playing, especially on rough or uneven surfaces. This discomfort can lead to a lack of activity and reluctance to exercise, which could impact your dog's overall health.

Taking the time to care for your dog's paw pads through proper moisturizing, cleaning, and maintenance can prevent many of these problems, allowing your dog to move comfortably and stay healthy.

Signs of Paw Pad Issues

Before delving into the techniques for paw pad care, it's essential to understand the signs that your dog's paws may need attention.

Regularly inspecting your dog's paws will help you catch potential problems early and address them before they escalate. Some common signs that indicate a problem with your dog's paw pads include:

- **Cracked, Dry, or Flaky Skin**: If your dog's paws feel rough to the touch or appear cracked and dry, this is a sign that their paw pads are not getting enough moisture.
- **Redness or Swelling**: If the skin on your dog's paw pads appears red or swollen, this could be a sign of irritation, infection, or an allergic reaction.
- **Limping or Avoiding Walking**: If your dog is limping, refusing to walk, or seems to be favoring one paw, it may indicate that they are in pain due to a paw pad injury or irritation.
- **Discharge or Bleeding**: Any signs of fluid, pus, or blood coming from your dog's paw pads should be addressed immediately, as this may indicate an infection or injury.
- **Excessive Licking or Biting**: Dogs often lick or bite their paws when they are experiencing discomfort. If your dog is constantly licking or chewing their paw pads, it could be a sign of dryness, irritation, or infection.

By closely monitoring your dog's paw pads for these signs, you can address issues early and prevent further discomfort or complications.

Paw Pad Moisturizing: Why It's Important

Moisturizing your dog's paw pads is crucial to keeping them healthy and preventing cracks and dryness. Just like the skin on their body, your dog's paws can dry out, especially in certain environmental conditions. During winter, the cold air can strip moisture from their paws, while the hot summer sun or walking on hot pavement can cause burns or further dryness. Regular moisturizing helps to restore and maintain the natural balance of oils in your dog's paw pads, ensuring they stay soft, pliable, and protected.

Best Moisturizing Products for Paw Pads

Choosing the right moisturizing products for your dog's paw pads is essential for ensuring the health and comfort of their paws. Not all moisturizers are created equal, so it's important to select those that are specifically designed for dogs and free from harmful chemicals or fragrances.

Dog Paw Balms

Paw balms are specially formulated to help moisturize and protect your dog's paw pads. These balms are made from natural ingredients such as beeswax, shea butter, coconut oil, and essential oils that help soothe dry, cracked paw pads. Paw balms are applied directly to the pads and create a protective barrier against harsh elements, while also providing deep moisture.

Paw Wax

Paw wax is another popular product for moisturizing and protecting your dog's paws. Like paw balms, paw wax is made from natural ingredients and provides a protective coating that prevents damage from hot surfaces, cold snow, and rough terrains. Paw wax is particularly useful during extreme weather conditions, as it forms a thick layer of protection without being greasy.

Coconut Oil

Coconut oil is a natural, affordable option for moisturizing your dog's paw pads. Rich in fatty acids, coconut oil helps to soothe and hydrate dry skin while providing anti-inflammatory properties. It can be massaged into the paw pads, and many dogs enjoy the feeling of it. However, be cautious of your dog licking the oil, as too much consumption may upset their stomach.

Ointments and Creams

In addition to balms and waxes, you may want to consider using an ointment or cream that is designed specifically for dogs. These products usually contain soothing and healing ingredients like aloe vera, vitamin E, and calendula. They help promote healing in cracked or sore paw pads and prevent infections.

Techniques for Moisturizing Your Dog's Paw Pads

Once you've selected the right product, it's time to moisturize your dog's paws. Follow these steps to ensure you're providing the best care:

Step 1: Clean the Paw Pads

Before applying any moisturizer, make sure your dog's paws are clean and dry. Gently wash your dog's paw pads with warm water and mild pet-safe soap, ensuring that any dirt, debris, or salt from winter roads is removed. Pat the paws dry with a clean towel.

Step 2: Apply Moisturizer

Once the paw pads are clean and dry, apply a generous amount of your chosen moisturizer (balm, wax, or cream) to the pads. Use your fingers to gently massage the product into the paw pads and between the toes, ensuring that the moisturizer is absorbed evenly.

Step 3: Massage for Absorption

Massaging the moisturizer into the paw pads not only helps the product absorb but also provides a calming, bonding experience for you and your dog. The gentle pressure of the massage will also increase circulation, which is beneficial for the health of your dog's paws.

Step 4: Allow Time to Absorb

After applying the moisturizer, give your dog time to allow the product to fully absorb. Avoid allowing your dog to walk on rough surfaces immediately after applying the balm or cream, as it could rub off. If you need to, consider using protective booties for your dog to wear for a while to ensure the product stays in place.

Preventing Paw Pad Damage: Additional Tips

While moisturizing is crucial, there are other important tips to help prevent paw pad damage:

- **Regular Inspection**: Regularly check your dog's paws for signs of wear and tear, such as cracks, abrasions, or foreign objects stuck between the pads. Early detection can prevent more severe issues.
- **Avoid Hot Pavement**: During hot weather, avoid walking your dog on pavement or asphalt, as these surfaces can burn

their paw pads. Walk your dog in the early morning or late evening when temperatures are cooler.

- **Protective Booties**: If your dog's paws are particularly sensitive or if you're walking on rough terrain, consider using protective booties. These booties will provide an extra layer of protection from harsh surfaces and prevent damage to the paw pads.
- **Paw Pad Trimming**: Keep the hair around your dog's paws trimmed to prevent matting and reduce the chances of debris becoming trapped in the pads.
- **Hydration**: Just as hydration is important for your dog's overall health, it also helps keep their paws hydrated. Make sure your dog has access to fresh water throughout the day.

Caring for your dog's paw pads is an essential part of their overall health and well-being. Moisturizing the paw pads regularly and providing protective care in harsh conditions can help prevent pain, cracks, and injuries. By following the tips outlined in this section, you can ensure that your dog's paws remain healthy, strong, and comfortable. Taking the time to address paw pad issues and protect your dog's feet will not only improve their quality of life but also strengthen your bond with your furry companion as you care for them with love and attention.

Identifying and Treating Skin Conditions in Dogs

Your dog's skin is not only its largest organ but also a major indicator of its overall health. A healthy coat and skin reflect a dog that is generally in good condition. However, skin problems are one of the most common issues that pet owners face. Skin conditions in dogs can be caused by various factors such as allergies, infections, parasites, or underlying health problems. These issues can range from mild irritations to serious conditions that may require veterinary attention. Recognizing skin conditions early on and taking prompt action can help ensure your dog remains comfortable and healthy.

In this section, we'll explore the most common skin conditions in dogs, how to identify them, and effective treatments to address these issues. We will also discuss preventative measures and the importance of proper skincare to maintain your dog's skin health. Whether you're dealing with a minor rash or more complex dermatological issues, understanding the symptoms and treatments of skin conditions is key to providing the best care for your dog.

Common Dog Skin Conditions

Skin conditions in dogs can manifest in many different ways, including rashes, lumps, bumps, hair loss, scabs, itching, and inflammation. Here are some of the most common skin conditions that affect dogs:

Allergies

Allergies are one of the most frequent causes of skin problems in dogs. Just like humans, dogs can suffer from allergic reactions to various environmental factors, food, or substances they come into contact with. Common allergens for dogs include:

- **Flea bites**: Flea allergy dermatitis (FAD) occurs when a dog becomes hypersensitive to the saliva of fleas. The dog may experience severe itching, hair loss, red spots, and scabs.
- **Food allergies**: Dogs can develop allergies to certain ingredients in their food, such as beef, chicken, dairy, or

grains. These allergies can cause itching, ear infections, and gastrointestinal problems.
- **Environmental allergens**: Pollens, dust mites, mold, and grasses can trigger allergies in dogs, especially during peak allergy seasons. This type of allergy is often seasonal but can also occur year-round.

Flea Infestation and Flea Allergies

Fleas are one of the most common external parasites that cause skin problems in dogs. Flea infestations lead to intense itching, hair loss, redness, and the formation of scabs and sores. Flea allergy dermatitis (FAD) occurs when a dog has an allergic reaction to the flea's saliva. This condition leads to severe itching and can result in the dog scratching, biting, and licking the affected areas excessively. Fleas can also transmit other parasites such as tapeworms, adding to the complexity of treatment.

Hot Spots (Pyotraumatic Dermatitis)

Hot spots are areas of infected, inflamed skin that develop when a dog constantly licks, chews, or scratches a particular spot. The excessive licking causes the skin to break down, leading to an infection. These hotspots are typically moist, red, and very painful. Hot spots are often caused by allergies, flea infestations, or other underlying skin conditions that make the dog's skin vulnerable to secondary infections.

Dry Skin and Dandruff

Dry, flaky skin and dandruff are common in dogs, especially during the winter months when the air is dry. Itchiness, scaling, and flaking of the skin can be caused by environmental factors, dehydration, or underlying medical conditions. Dry skin can lead to discomfort for your dog, and if left untreated, it can result in infections or secondary skin problems. Dogs with dry skin may also develop an oily coat, which can make their fur appear greasy.

Ringworm (Dermatophytosis)

Ringworm is a fungal infection that can cause circular patches of hair loss, often with a scaly, crusty appearance. Despite its name, ringworm is not caused by worms but by fungi that affect the skin, hair, and nails. Dogs with compromised immune systems or those in close contact with other infected animals are at higher risk of contracting ringworm. Treatment usually involves antifungal medications and topical treatments.

Mange

Mange is a skin condition caused by parasitic mites that burrow into the skin, causing severe itching, hair loss, redness, and scabbing. There are two main types of mange:

- **Sarcoptic Mange (Scabies)**: Caused by the Sarcoptes scabiei mite, this form of mange is highly contagious and can affect other animals and humans. It leads to intense itching, hair loss, and scabbing.
- **Demodectic Mange (Demodicosis)**: Caused by the Demodex mite, this type of mange is typically not contagious. It is often seen in puppies or dogs with weakened immune systems and can result in hair loss and secondary bacterial infections.

Skin Infections (Bacterial and Fungal)

Skin infections can occur when bacteria or fungi enter the skin through broken or damaged areas. Bacterial infections are often caused by opportunistic bacteria like Staphylococcus, which takes advantage of the body's weakened defenses, often due to allergies, poor hygiene, or other skin conditions. These infections can cause redness, swelling, pustules, and odor. Fungal infections, including yeast infections, can cause itching, redness, and a musty odor, often affecting the ears, paws, and skin folds.

Sebaceous Cysts

Sebaceous cysts are fluid-filled lumps that form beneath the skin when a sebaceous gland becomes blocked. These cysts are usually benign, but they can cause irritation if they rupture or become infected. Sebaceous cysts are common in certain breeds and may appear as soft, movable lumps under the skin. If a cyst becomes infected or painful, it may need to be drained or surgically removed by a veterinarian.

Skin Tumors

Although many skin tumors are benign, they can still cause concern due to their size or location. Common skin tumors in dogs include lipomas (benign fatty tumors) and mast cell tumors. While some tumors may remain harmless, others, such as malignant mast cell tumors, can be aggressive and require surgical intervention and treatment. It's essential to have any new growths on your dog's skin evaluated by a veterinarian to determine the best course of action.

Identifying Skin Conditions in Dogs

Recognizing a skin problem early can make treatment more effective and prevent further complications. Here are some common signs that your dog may have a skin condition:

- **Excessive Scratching, Licking, or Biting**: If your dog is constantly scratching, licking, or biting at certain areas of its body, it could indicate itching caused by allergies, fleas, or dry skin.
- **Redness or Inflammation**: Inflamed, red skin is often a sign of infection, allergies, or irritants. This is typically accompanied by swelling or heat in the affected area.
- **Hair Loss**: Hair loss is a common symptom of various skin conditions, including mange, fungal infections, or flea infestations. Bald patches may appear in specific areas, especially if your dog is scratching or biting the affected region.
- **Scabs, Sores, and Bumps**: Scabs and sores often develop due to continuous scratching or biting. They can result from flea bites, allergies, or secondary infections. Bumps can also form as a result of cysts, abscesses, or tumors.
- **Odor**: A strong, unpleasant odor coming from your dog's skin or coat may indicate a fungal or bacterial infection.
- **Skin Discoloration**: Skin conditions can cause changes in the color or texture of your dog's skin. Darkened skin may indicate chronic irritation or fungal infections, while pale or discolored patches could be a sign of an underlying issue.
- **Flaky or Dry Skin**: Dry, flaky skin or dandruff is often a sign of an underlying problem such as dry air, allergies, or poor nutrition.

Treating Skin Conditions in Dogs

Treatment for skin conditions in dogs depends on the underlying cause. Below are some general approaches to treating common skin problems:

Topical Treatments

Topical treatments, such as creams, ointments, and sprays, can help soothe inflamed skin, reduce itching, and prevent infection. These treatments may contain ingredients like hydrocortisone, aloe vera, or antifungal agents to address specific skin issues. Always consult your veterinarian before using over-the-counter products to ensure they are safe for your dog.

Medications

For more severe or persistent skin conditions, medications may be necessary. Oral antihistamines, corticosteroids, or antibiotics can be prescribed to treat allergies, infections, or inflammation. For fungal infections like ringworm, antifungal medications may be required.

Flea and Tick Prevention

If fleas are causing your dog's skin issues, effective flea control products such as topical treatments, oral medications, or flea collars are essential. Regular flea prevention is key to avoiding flea infestations and flea allergy dermatitis.

Bathing with Medicated Shampoos

Medicated shampoos designed for dogs can help alleviate symptoms of skin conditions. These shampoos may contain ingredients such as chlorhexidine, sulfur, or oatmeal to soothe the skin, reduce inflammation, and eliminate bacteria or fungi. It's important to use shampoos specifically formulated for dogs, as human shampoos can irritate their skin.

Dietary Changes

If your dog has food allergies, switching to a hypoallergenic or limited ingredient diet may help resolve skin issues. Omega-3 fatty acids, found in fish oils, can also improve skin health and reduce inflammation.

Regular Grooming

Regular grooming, including brushing, can help prevent mats, tangles, and buildup of allergens in your dog's coat. It also promotes healthy skin by improving blood circulation and distributing natural oils throughout the coat.

Veterinary Consultation

In severe cases or when symptoms persist, it is essential to consult a veterinarian. A vet can perform diagnostic tests to identify the underlying cause of the skin issue and recommend the most effective treatment plan.

Preventing Skin Conditions

The best way to deal with skin conditions is to prevent them from occurring in the first place. Here are some tips for maintaining healthy skin and coat for your dog:

- **Regular Grooming**: Regular brushing, bathing, and checking for parasites can help maintain healthy skin and coat.
- **Balanced Diet**: A nutritious diet rich in essential fatty acids and vitamins is crucial for skin health. Consider incorporating supplements like fish oil to support your dog's skin.
- **Flea Prevention**: Use flea prevention products regularly to avoid flea infestations.
- **Moisturize**: In dry or cold weather, use pet-safe moisturizers on your dog's skin to prevent dryness and cracking.

By staying proactive with your dog's skincare routine, you can reduce the likelihood of skin conditions and provide your furry friend with the comfort and care they need. Regular monitoring, early identification, and prompt treatment are key to managing skin health effectively.

Chapter 5: Specialized Grooming

Specialized grooming goes beyond the basics of regular coat care, focusing on the unique grooming needs of different breeds, specific conditions, and dogs with special requirements. While all dogs require regular grooming to maintain their health and appearance, certain dogs have specific grooming demands due to their coat type, size, or health status.

Whether you have a long-haired breed that requires intricate grooming or a dog with a medical condition that affects their coat or skin, specialized grooming ensures they receive the best care suited to their needs.

In this chapter, we will explore the various aspects of specialized grooming, including techniques for grooming hypoallergenic breeds, senior dogs, and puppies, as well as grooming tips for dogs with physical disabilities or medical conditions.

Additionally, we will cover breed-specific grooming practices, such as those for dogs with double coats, curly coats, or non-shedding coats. Specialized grooming requires attention to detail and an understanding of each dog's unique characteristics, making it an essential skill for every pet owner.

Whether you're preparing for a show, addressing health issues, or simply ensuring that your dog's grooming routine is tailored to their needs, this chapter will guide you through the specialized care that keeps your dog healthy, happy, and looking their best.

Grooming Puppies: A Gentle Start

Grooming is an essential part of a puppy's growth and development, and starting this routine early is crucial for building trust, comfort, and a positive association with grooming. Establishing good grooming habits in a puppy's formative months helps them become accustomed to being handled, reduces stress during grooming sessions, and ensures they grow up to be well-groomed, healthy adults. However, puppy grooming requires a different approach from grooming adult dogs. Since puppies are more sensitive to handling and their skin is more delicate, it's important to take a gentle, gradual approach to avoid overwhelming them.

Why Start Grooming Early?

Starting grooming as early as possible gives puppies the opportunity to become familiar with various grooming tools and processes. Early grooming also helps with their socialization, teaching them how to relax and trust you when being touched. This is especially beneficial for breeds or individual dogs that may be prone to nervousness or anxiety around grooming. By handling their paws, ears, coat, and teeth early on, you create positive experiences that can last a lifetime. Grooming at a young age helps puppies to grow accustomed to various tools like brushes, clippers, and scissors, making future grooming sessions easier for both the puppy and the owner.

Additionally, grooming puppies regularly promotes overall health. It allows you to check for signs of skin infections, parasites like fleas or ticks, or any abnormal bumps and growths. As you're handling your puppy, you can also get to know their body, making it easier to spot any changes that might indicate health issues.

Gradual Introduction to Grooming Tools

Since puppies are more sensitive to new experiences, it's essential to start grooming with a gentle approach and avoid overwhelming them with too many new things at once. Begin by introducing the grooming tools slowly, allowing the puppy to get used to the sight, sound, and feel of each one. For example:

- **Brushes**: Start with a soft brush that is comfortable on their delicate skin. Lightly brush your puppy for just a few minutes, allowing them to get used to the sensation. Gradually increase the brushing time as they become more accustomed to it.
- **Clippers**: Noise can be unsettling for puppies, so start by getting them familiar with the sound of the clippers before using them on their coat. You can do this by running the clippers near them without touching their skin, letting them get used to the noise. When it's time to trim their fur, start slowly, using a guard to avoid cutting too close to their skin.
- **Scissors**: Some puppies may be intimidated by the sight of scissors, so make sure to show them the scissors without using them right away. Gently introduce the scissors into your routine as you trim small sections of their coat.
- **Nail Trimmers**: Nail trimming can be one of the most challenging grooming tasks for puppies. Begin by gently handling their paws, touching each toe to get them used to being touched. Then, gradually introduce the nail trimmers, trimming only the tip of one nail at a time. Keep each session short and rewarding.

Bathing Puppies

Bathing is another important part of the puppy grooming process, but it's essential to use a gentle approach, as puppies have sensitive skin. Start by getting your puppy used to being in a bathtub or sink. Let them explore the area before introducing water, and make sure to use lukewarm water to prevent them from getting chilled or overheated.

When it comes to shampoo, use a mild, puppy-safe formula designed specifically for their sensitive skin. Avoid using harsh human shampoos, as they can strip natural oils from a puppy's coat and cause dryness or irritation. Be gentle when lathering the shampoo and avoid getting water or soap in their eyes, ears, or nose. To make the experience more enjoyable for your puppy, keep bath time short and calm, speaking to them in soothing tones throughout the process.

After the bath, gently pat your puppy dry with a soft towel, and use a blow dryer on the lowest heat setting if necessary to dry their coat. However, not all puppies will tolerate a blow dryer, so it's important to observe their comfort level and find alternative methods if they are scared.

Brushing and Coat Maintenance

Regular brushing is essential for a puppy's coat health. Even if your puppy has a short coat, brushing is still necessary to prevent the buildup of dirt, debris, and loose fur. For puppies with long or thick coats, brushing helps to prevent matting and tangles and encourages the development of healthy hair.

To begin brushing your puppy, use a soft-bristled brush or a puppy-specific brush that is gentle on their delicate skin. Be patient and start with small sections of their coat, brushing in the direction of hair growth. Ensure that brushing sessions are calm and positive, stopping frequently for short breaks if needed. Over time, your puppy will become more accustomed to brushing and will enjoy the process as part of their routine.

For puppies with longer coats, introduce detangling sprays or conditioners that are safe for puppies to help prevent tangling and matting. Be extra careful when brushing around sensitive areas such as the face, ears, and paws. Gently lift the fur and work through any tangles with your fingers before brushing through with the brush.

Socialization and Handling

Grooming is also an excellent opportunity to socialize your puppy and build their confidence. Regular handling—touching their paws, ears, tail, and face—helps them get used to being touched in different ways. This is important for future vet visits, where handling and being examined will be necessary. Start by touching their ears, teeth, and paws daily to get them accustomed to these areas being handled. Use praise and treats to create positive associations with these activities.

Additionally, expose your puppy to other grooming environments, such as dog groomers or busy areas, to help them become comfortable in new situations. You can practice by taking them for walks in new places or arranging playdates with other well-behaved dogs to help them learn how to interact with other animals and humans in different environments.

Nail Care for Puppies

Nail trimming can be an intimidating task for puppies, but it's essential to start early to prevent overgrowth and discomfort. Begin by gently massaging your puppy's paws and getting them used to having their nails touched. This makes the actual trimming process easier as they get accustomed to the sensation. Use a puppy-specific nail clipper with rounded edges to prevent accidents, and trim only the tips of their nails. Be sure to trim a little at a time to avoid cutting into the quick, which can be painful and cause bleeding.

During the first few nail trims, keep sessions short and sweet, offering praise and treats afterward to reinforce positive behavior. Gradually increase the frequency of nail trims as your puppy becomes more comfortable with the process.

Creating a Positive Grooming Experience

The key to grooming puppies is to make it a positive, gentle, and enjoyable experience. Use treats, praise, and calm reassurance to help your puppy associate grooming with something pleasant. Avoid forcing the puppy into uncomfortable situations, as this can lead to fear and anxiety around grooming in the future. If your puppy seems overwhelmed or frightened, take a break and try again later, gradually increasing the length and complexity of grooming sessions as they grow older and become more accustomed to the routine.

Patience and consistency are key in grooming puppies. By starting early, using positive reinforcement, and handling them gently, you're setting your puppy up for a lifetime of good grooming habits. With time, your puppy will grow accustomed to the process and enjoy their grooming sessions, helping to maintain their health and well-being throughout their life.

Grooming Older Dogs and Dogs with Special Needs

As dogs age or develop special needs, their grooming requirements evolve, and it becomes crucial to tailor grooming routines to accommodate these changes. Older dogs and dogs with special needs, whether due to medical conditions, disabilities, or physical limitations, may require extra care, patience, and a gentle touch during grooming sessions. With proper care, these dogs can remain comfortable, clean, and healthy as they navigate their later years or cope with challenges that affect their mobility and health. This extended content will explore the essential grooming practices for older dogs and dogs with special needs, ensuring they are treated with the care and respect they deserve.

Understanding the Needs of Older Dogs

As dogs get older, they may experience various physical and health changes that can impact their grooming needs. Understanding these changes is vital to ensuring that your senior dog feels comfortable during grooming and remains in the best possible health. Some common age-related changes include:

- **Decreased mobility**: Older dogs may struggle to move around as easily as they once did. They might have arthritis or joint pain, which can make grooming tasks such as nail trimming, bathing, and even brushing more difficult.
- **Thinning or changing coat**: As dogs age, their coat may become thinner or change texture. Some dogs may shed more, while others may have a harder time maintaining their coat, leading to matting and tangling.
- **Drier skin**: Senior dogs often experience drier skin, which can lead to itching, flaking, or overall discomfort. This can

make regular bathing and moisturizing an essential part of their grooming routine.
- **Sensory changes**: Older dogs may also experience sensory changes that affect their ability to hear or see. For example, they might not hear the sound of the clippers or may be startled by sudden movements or noises. These factors must be considered when grooming to reduce anxiety and stress.
- **Health conditions**: Older dogs are more prone to various health issues, such as dental problems, vision and hearing loss, skin infections, and more. These issues often require special attention during grooming sessions.

By recognizing and accommodating these changes, you can ensure that your senior dog's grooming routine supports their overall health and well-being.

Creating a Comfortable Grooming Environment for Senior Dogs

When grooming an older dog, comfort is key. Make sure the environment is calm and stress-free, as older dogs may be more sensitive to noise, movement, or abrupt handling. Follow these tips to create an ideal grooming space:

- **Choose a quiet, calm location**: Select a quiet room free from distractions where your dog can relax during grooming. This can help reduce anxiety and make the experience more pleasant.
- **Use a non-slip mat**: If your dog has trouble standing due to arthritis or other mobility issues, place a non-slip mat on the grooming table or floor to prevent slipping. This will help them feel more stable and comfortable while being groomed.

- **Provide support**: If your dog is large or heavy, you may need assistance lifting them onto a grooming table or bath. For smaller dogs, use a low platform or grooming table that allows them to easily climb onto it without straining their joints.
- **Take breaks**: Senior dogs may have shorter attention spans or become fatigued quickly. If your dog shows signs of stress, discomfort, or fatigue, take breaks during grooming sessions. Go slow, and don't rush through any process.
- **Keep the space well-lit**: If your dog has vision issues, make sure the grooming area is well-lit to help them feel more at ease and avoid any surprises during grooming.

Brushing and Coat Care for Senior Dogs

Older dogs may require extra attention when it comes to brushing and coat care. The process of brushing not only helps maintain a healthy coat but also provides a bonding experience and a way to check for skin problems, parasites, or other health issues. Brushing your senior dog regularly can also help prevent mats and tangles, which can be more uncomfortable for older dogs. However, the approach to brushing may differ depending on their coat type, age-related sensitivities, and mobility limitations.

- **Gentle brushing**: Use gentle brushes and combs designed for sensitive skin. Choose a soft-bristle brush or a comb with wide-spaced teeth to avoid hurting your dog or pulling on their hair. For dogs with fine coats, a pin brush or slicker brush may work well, but be careful not to press too hard on their skin.
- **Avoid matting**: As senior dogs age, they may have difficulty grooming themselves properly. This can lead to mats or

tangles, especially in long-haired breeds. You may need to pay extra attention to areas where mats are most likely to form, such as behind the ears, around the collar area, and under the legs. If mats are difficult to remove, you may need to seek professional grooming assistance.
- **Consider the dog's coat changes**: As a dog's coat changes with age, they may shed more than they used to. You may notice that the coat becomes thinner in certain areas, especially on the back, sides, or legs. Regular brushing helps remove dead hair and promotes blood circulation to the skin, keeping it healthy.
- **Handle sensitivities gently**: Older dogs may have sensitive areas or spots that are more prone to discomfort or irritation. If your dog has arthritis or joint pain, you may need to be more cautious when brushing near their limbs, tail, or back. Work around sore spots gently and stop if your dog appears to be in pain.

Bathing Older Dogs

Bathing is a crucial part of your senior dog's grooming routine, but it may require extra care and attention to detail. Many older dogs have drier skin and may become easily chilled during bath time. Here are some tips for bathing older dogs:

- **Lukewarm water**: Use lukewarm water for bathing to avoid making your dog uncomfortable. Extreme temperatures, whether too hot or too cold, can be harsh on your dog's skin and joints.
- **Mild, moisturizing shampoo**: Choose a gentle, moisturizing dog shampoo that is suitable for senior dogs. Look for products designed to soothe dry skin and prevent

itching or irritation. Avoid using human shampoos, as they can dry out the skin and strip the coat of its natural oils.
- **Take extra care when rinsing**: Rinse your dog thoroughly to ensure that no shampoo or conditioner residue remains on their coat. Leftover product can cause irritation or dryness, particularly for senior dogs with sensitive skin.
- **Drying**: Dry your dog gently with a towel, patting rather than rubbing the coat. Use a blow dryer on the lowest setting if your dog tolerates it, but be mindful not to overheat them. Some senior dogs may be more sensitive to heat, so always check their comfort levels.

Nail Trimming for Senior Dogs

Nail trimming is a vital part of grooming for older dogs, but it can sometimes be more challenging. As dogs age, their nails can become thicker, and their growth may slow down. However, neglected nails can cause discomfort or even lead to joint problems or difficulty walking. For older dogs, nail trimming should be done regularly, and extra care should be taken to avoid causing pain or injury.

- **Use the right tools**: For senior dogs, choose a high-quality, sharp nail clipper that can cut through thicker nails without causing cracks or splits. You can also use a grinder to smooth rough edges and shorten the nails.
- **Take it slow**: Older dogs may be more sensitive to having their paws touched or manipulated. Go slow, take frequent breaks, and never force the nail trimming process. If your dog becomes stressed or anxious, stop and try again later.
- **Check the nails regularly**: Make it a habit to check your dog's nails weekly, even if they don't seem long. As dogs age, they may not wear down their nails as effectively

through regular walking, so trimming may be needed more often than when they were younger.

Dental Care for Senior Dogs

Dental health is just as important for senior dogs as it is for younger ones. Dental problems such as tartar buildup, gum disease, and tooth decay can affect older dogs, leading to pain, difficulty eating, or even systemic health issues. Regular brushing, dental checkups, and professional cleanings are crucial for maintaining oral health in senior dogs.

- **Brushing**: Brush your dog's teeth with a dog-specific toothbrush and toothpaste, ideally on a regular basis. For older dogs, it may be helpful to start slowly and gradually get them accustomed to the brushing routine.
- **Dental treats**: Consider providing dental chews or treats designed to help remove plaque and tartar. These can be especially helpful for senior dogs that may not tolerate regular tooth brushing.
- **Routine veterinary checkups**: Regular vet visits are essential for identifying and treating dental issues early. Older dogs may develop gum disease, tooth abscesses, or other conditions that require professional care.

Special Considerations for Dogs with Disabilities or Health Conditions

Dogs with physical disabilities or health conditions, such as arthritis, visual or hearing impairments, or mobility challenges, may need extra assistance during grooming. Some dogs may be unable to climb into a bath or stand on a grooming table, while others may be frightened or disoriented due to vision or hearing loss. The following tips will help you care for these dogs while grooming them:

- **Arthritis and mobility issues**: Use ramps or steps to help dogs with arthritis or mobility challenges reach grooming areas. Use non-slip mats and offer additional support while brushing or trimming their nails. Take extra care when lifting or handling them.
- **Dogs with vision or hearing impairments**: Use touch and voice commands to reassure dogs with sensory impairments. Make sure the grooming area is quiet, and approach the dog gently so as not to startle them.
- **Medical conditions**: If your dog has a medical condition that affects their skin, such as skin infections or rashes, avoid using harsh shampoos or grooming products. Consult your veterinarian for guidance on appropriate products and care techniques.

Grooming older dogs and dogs with special needs requires patience, understanding, and a compassionate approach. By modifying grooming routines to suit their physical limitations and health challenges, you can ensure that they continue to feel comfortable, safe, and cared for. Always consult with a veterinarian if you're unsure about how to handle your dog's grooming needs, and be prepared to adapt your approach as your dog's age or condition changes over time.

Grooming for Dogs with Medical Conditions

Grooming is a crucial part of a dog's health routine, especially for those with medical conditions. While grooming can sometimes be a source of discomfort for dogs, it's also an important tool for monitoring their health and preventing further issues. For dogs with specific health conditions, grooming can be a little more involved. Medical conditions can affect the dog's skin, coat, behavior, and mobility, which may require customized grooming practices. Whether your dog has a chronic condition like arthritis, a skin disorder, or a specific disease, it is essential to approach grooming with care, patience, and specialized techniques to ensure their comfort and health. This comprehensive content will explore the best practices and considerations for grooming dogs with various medical conditions.

The Importance of Grooming for Dogs with Medical Conditions

For dogs with medical conditions, grooming is not just about keeping them clean and tidy; it also plays an integral role in monitoring their health. The process of grooming can reveal signs of illnesses, infections, or injuries that may go unnoticed in everyday life. Regular grooming also provides an opportunity to bond with your dog and help them feel comfortable and cared for, despite any challenges they may be facing. For dogs with health issues, grooming can provide therapeutic benefits as well, such as increased blood circulation, which is essential for overall health.

- **Detecting health problems**: Regular grooming allows you to keep an eye out for health issues like skin infections, lumps, bumps, ticks, and changes in coat texture. Early

detection of these issues can help prevent complications and support treatment.
- **Monitoring medications**: Grooming can help you track any changes in your dog's response to medications, especially for conditions like skin infections or hormonal imbalances that affect coat health.
- **Supporting mobility**: Many medical conditions impact a dog's ability to move freely. Grooming routines can be adjusted to support their movement limitations, ensuring that they don't experience pain or stress during the process.

Grooming Dogs with Skin Conditions

Dogs with skin conditions, such as allergies, dermatitis, fungal infections, or hot spots, require special attention during grooming. Depending on the specific condition, there may be a need for gentle handling, medicated shampoos, or specific techniques to avoid further irritation or damage to the skin. Here's how to approach grooming for dogs with various skin conditions:

1. Allergies and Dermatitis

Allergies can cause dogs to experience itching, inflammation, and discomfort. Dermatitis, which is often caused by allergies, can result in red, inflamed, and irritated skin. Dogs suffering from these conditions may also be prone to dry skin, flaking, or even hair loss.

- **Use hypoallergenic products**: Choose shampoos and conditioners that are specifically formulated for dogs with sensitive skin. These products are typically free of fragrances, dyes, and harsh chemicals, all of which can worsen allergic reactions.

- **Regular bathing with medicated shampoo**: Bathing your dog regularly with a medicated shampoo can help soothe the skin and provide relief from itching. Ensure that you follow the veterinarian's recommendations for the frequency of bathing and the appropriate product.
- **Gentle brushing**: Use a soft-bristled brush or comb to avoid irritating the skin. Brushing can help remove allergens from the coat and reduce the risk of flare-ups.
- **Pay attention to specific areas**: Areas like the paws, ears, and belly may be more prone to irritation, so be extra gentle when handling these parts of the body.

2. Hot Spots and Fungal Infections

Hot spots (acute moist dermatitis) are painful, inflamed areas of the skin that can result from excessive licking, scratching, or moisture buildup. These can lead to secondary bacterial or fungal infections, which require immediate attention.

- **Avoid touching irritated areas**: When grooming, try to avoid touching hot spots or any inflamed areas to prevent further irritation. Consult your veterinarian for appropriate treatment and care instructions.
- **Medicated baths**: For fungal infections or hot spots, use an antifungal or antibacterial shampoo recommended by your vet. These shampoos can help treat the underlying infection and prevent it from worsening.
- **Moisturizing the skin**: After bathing, use a vet-approved moisturizer to keep the skin hydrated and prevent further irritation. Dry, cracked skin can be painful, so moisturizing is essential for healing.

- **Dry thoroughly**: Hot spots and fungal infections thrive in moist environments. Ensure that your dog's coat and skin are thoroughly dried after a bath to reduce the risk of fungal or bacterial overgrowth.

3. Eczema and Dry Skin

Eczema, which causes red, itchy, and inflamed skin, can affect dogs of all ages. Dogs with dry skin may also experience scaling, flaking, and discomfort. Grooming for dogs with eczema or dry skin requires gentle handling and the use of moisturizing products.

- **Use hydrating shampoos**: Look for shampoos with moisturizing ingredients such as oatmeal, aloe vera, and shea butter. These can help soothe dry and irritated skin.
- **Avoid over-bathing**: Bathing your dog too frequently can strip the skin of its natural oils. Limit baths to only when necessary and use a gentle, moisturizing shampoo to help maintain skin hydration.
- **Topical treatments**: After grooming, your vet may recommend topical creams or oils to alleviate dryness and itching. These treatments can help restore moisture to the skin and promote healing.

Grooming Dogs with Mobility Challenges

Mobility challenges, such as arthritis, hip dysplasia, or neurological conditions, can make it difficult for dogs to stand or move around during grooming. Dogs with mobility limitations require extra care and support to ensure they remain comfortable and safe during grooming sessions. Here are a few tips for grooming dogs with mobility issues:

- **Use ramps or steps**: If your dog has difficulty jumping or climbing, use a ramp or steps to help them reach the grooming table or bathtub. Ramps and steps will minimize strain on their joints and help them feel more secure.
- **Opt for low-impact grooming**: For dogs with arthritis or joint pain, limit the time spent standing or moving. Use a grooming table with adjustable height to reduce strain on your dog's body, or groom them on the floor if they are unable to stand for long periods.
- **Frequent breaks**: If your dog has difficulty remaining still, take frequent breaks during grooming sessions. Allow them to stretch their legs, move around, and rest as needed.
- **Massage during grooming**: Gently massaging your dog's muscles during grooming can help improve circulation and relieve tension. This can be especially beneficial for dogs with arthritis or muscle stiffness.

Grooming Dogs with Chronic Health Conditions

Chronic health conditions, such as diabetes, hypothyroidism, or kidney disease, can affect the dog's energy levels, coat quality, and overall grooming needs. Grooming for dogs with chronic conditions often requires adjustments in technique to accommodate their condition.

1. Diabetes

Dogs with diabetes often have changes in their coat, skin, and overall health. Grooming can help manage these changes and provide additional health benefits.

- **Monitor coat quality**: Dogs with diabetes may experience hair loss or thinning coats. Brush regularly to promote blood circulation and remove loose hair.
- **Take care around sores or infections**: Diabetic dogs are prone to skin infections and sores, so be extra cautious when grooming to avoid aggravating these areas.
- **Watch for dehydration**: Diabetes can cause dehydration, leading to dry skin. Make sure to moisturize your dog's skin and provide plenty of fresh water.

2. Hypothyroidism

Hypothyroidism in dogs can cause symptoms such as hair loss, dry skin, and a dull coat. These changes can make grooming more difficult, but regular care can help maintain skin and coat health.

- **Use moisturizing products**: Hypothyroid dogs often experience dry, flaky skin, so regular moisturizing is crucial. Use shampoos with hydrating ingredients and conditioners to restore moisture.
- **Regular brushing**: Brushing your dog regularly helps remove dead hair and stimulates blood circulation to the skin, which is important for coat health.

3. Kidney Disease

Dogs with kidney disease may experience changes in their coat and skin due to dehydration, protein loss, and other complications. Grooming for dogs with kidney disease should be gentle and focused on comfort.

- **Frequent brushing**: Kidney disease can cause the coat to become dry and brittle. Regular brushing helps remove dead hair and stimulates the skin.
- **Gentle baths**: Use a gentle, moisturizing shampoo to avoid stripping essential oils from the skin. Bathe your dog only as needed, and avoid prolonged exposure to water.

Grooming for Dogs with Visual or Hearing Impairments

Dogs with sensory impairments, such as blindness or deafness, may be more sensitive during grooming. These dogs may have heightened senses of touch, smell, or hearing, making it important to approach grooming in a way that minimizes anxiety and discomfort.

- **Use touch and scent cues**: Blind or visually impaired dogs rely on their sense of touch to understand their environment. Use soft, calming touch during grooming to reassure them. For deaf dogs, voice cues may not be effective, so try using hand signals or visual cues to communicate during grooming.
- **Keep noise to a minimum**: Deaf dogs may be startled by loud noises, such as the sound of clippers or a blow dryer. Try to use quieter grooming tools or work in a space where loud noises can be minimized.
- **Consistency and patience**: Both blind and deaf dogs may become anxious if their grooming routine changes. Consistency and patience are essential for ensuring a calm grooming experience.

Grooming for dogs with medical conditions requires extra attention, care, and understanding of their unique needs. Whether it's managing skin conditions, mobility issues, or chronic health concerns, adjusting grooming routines to suit the dog's condition will improve their quality of life and health.

Show Dog Grooming Standards

Show dog grooming is a meticulous and specialized practice designed to prepare dogs for competitive dog shows. The grooming process goes beyond mere cleanliness and style; it focuses on highlighting the breed's specific traits as outlined by the standards set by various kennel clubs and breed registries. Each dog breed has distinct features and qualities that are essential for showcasing its best attributes during competitions, and grooming plays a key role in achieving that goal. Understanding the show dog grooming standards is critical for anyone involved in the dog show scene, whether you're an owner, handler, or groomer.

The Importance of Show Dog Grooming

Show dog grooming is an art form that requires both skill and knowledge. The aim is to prepare the dog in a way that enhances its natural beauty while adhering to the breed's standard. The presentation of the dog reflects its health, cleanliness, and overall well-being. A well-groomed dog is seen as more polished, confident, and healthy, all of which can influence the judge's opinion in a competitive environment.

- **Breed Standard Alignment**: Each breed has a specific standard that outlines physical characteristics, coat types, colors, and overall appearance. Grooming helps to emphasize these features to ensure that the dog matches the ideal appearance for that breed.

- **Presentation**: A show dog's grooming should convey a sense of balance, symmetry, and correctness that enhances the dog's natural traits. Grooming is crucial to presenting a dog in its best light, increasing its chances of excelling in the competition.
- **Health and Well-being**: Grooming provides an opportunity to check the dog for any skin issues, parasites, or injuries that might go unnoticed. A healthy dog, with no signs of discomfort or irritation, stands a better chance of impressing the judge.

Understanding the Breed Standards

Each breed has its own specific grooming standards that are closely tied to its breed standard. These standards define everything from the coat type to the dog's physical characteristics and behavior. Show dog grooming requires a deep understanding of these standards to ensure that the grooming process aligns with the expectations for each breed.

- **Coat Type and Texture**: Depending on the breed, grooming may involve a variety of techniques to enhance the dog's coat. For example, breeds with long, silky coats, such as the Afghan Hound or Yorkshire Terrier, require careful trimming, brushing, and sometimes the use of specific styling products to maintain their luxurious appearance. Breeds with wiry coats, like the Wire Fox Terrier or Schnauzer, may need hand-stripping or specialized scissoring techniques to keep the coat in the right texture and shape.
- **Color and Pattern**: Show dogs are judged not only on their coat texture but also on the consistency of their color and the

correctness of any patterns that are specific to the breed. Proper grooming ensures that the coat's color is vibrant and free from discoloration. It may also involve techniques like light trimming or plucking to maintain specific color patterns and markings.

- **Conformation and Structure**: Grooming isn't only about appearance; it's also about ensuring the dog's conformation is in line with the breed standard. This means making sure the coat falls in a way that accentuates the dog's physical structure, such as the proper shape of the head, back, or legs. Proper grooming can help highlight these structural elements, presenting the dog at its best.

Grooming Requirements for Popular Show Breeds

Certain breeds are more commonly seen in the dog show ring, each with unique grooming requirements that align with their breed standard. Here are a few examples of popular show breeds and their grooming needs:

1. Poodles

Poodles are one of the most iconic breeds in dog shows, known for their distinctive coat and elegant appearance. Their grooming requirements are quite specific:

- **Coat Care**: Poodles have a dense, curly coat that must be meticulously maintained to avoid matting. Regular brushing is essential, and many show dogs have their coats clipped in a pattern that emphasizes their graceful movements and athletic build.

- **Specific Clips**: Poodles often wear a "continental clip" or "english saddle clip" for shows, which requires expertise to achieve the proper look. These styles involve shaving certain parts of the dog's body, leaving the legs and head fluffed to create a balanced and symmetrical appearance.
- **Ear Care**: Poodles' ears are prone to matting, and their grooming routine includes regular ear cleaning and trimming to ensure they remain neat and free from tangles.

2. Schnauzers

Schnauzers, particularly the Miniature Schnauzer and Standard Schnauzer, are known for their distinctive beards and eyebrows, which must be carefully shaped and trimmed to meet show standards.

- **Hand-stripping**: Schnauzers have a wiry coat that must be hand-stripped to maintain its texture. This involves plucking the dead hair from the coat to keep the coat firm and rough, as opposed to soft and floppy.
- **Facial Grooming**: The characteristic beard and eyebrows of the Schnauzer require special attention. The facial hair should be shaped carefully to enhance the dog's facial features while keeping the natural look.

3. Yorkshire Terriers

Yorkies are famous for their long, silky coats, which are a significant aspect of their breed standard. Show Yorkies require regular grooming to maintain the coat's sleek and polished appearance.

- **Brushing and Combing**: Yorkies need daily brushing to prevent tangles and mats in their fine hair. The coat should be combed thoroughly, especially in the areas prone to matting, like behind the ears and around the neck.
- **Trimming and Shaping**: While Yorkies are known for their long coats, some trimming may be necessary to maintain the ideal shape and prevent the coat from becoming overly long or unruly. A slight trim may be done around the face and ears to keep the dog looking neat and tidy.

4. Basset Hounds

Basset Hounds have a distinct look characterized by their droopy ears, long body, and short coat. While their grooming is less intricate than that of breeds with longer, more delicate coats, it still requires attention to specific areas.

- **Ear and Skin Care**: Basset Hounds' ears are long and prone to infections, so they must be cleaned regularly. The skin under the folds of their ears and around their eyes should also be kept clean and dry to prevent irritation.
- **Short Coat Maintenance**: Although Basset Hounds have short coats, they still require regular brushing to remove loose hair and maintain a healthy sheen. Bathing should be done as needed to keep the coat clean and free from odors.

Show Dog Grooming Techniques

The techniques used in show dog grooming vary depending on the breed and coat type, but some general principles apply to all dogs preparing for a competition.

- **Brushing**: Brushing is a fundamental part of show dog grooming, and it's essential for all dogs, regardless of coat type. Brushing removes tangles, mats, and loose hair, ensuring the coat remains sleek and shiny. The frequency and technique of brushing depend on the breed's coat type.
- **Bathing**: Bathing is essential for cleaning the coat and removing dirt, oils, and debris that can affect the dog's appearance. For show dogs, special shampoos and conditioners are often used to enhance the coat's shine and texture. Some breeds require specific products to maintain coat health, while others may need regular conditioning treatments to restore moisture and prevent dryness.
- **Trimming and Scissoring**: Dogs with long or thick coats may require regular trimming to keep their coats at the proper length and shape. Scissoring is often done to shape the coat, particularly for breeds with longer hair or specific breed standards that call for precise shaping.
- **Hand-stripping**: Some breeds with wiry coats, such as the Wire Fox Terrier or Schnauzer, require hand-stripping, which involves plucking the dead hair from the coat. This technique helps maintain the correct texture and color of the coat.
- **Ear and Nail Care**: In addition to coat grooming, show dogs require attention to their ears and nails. Regular ear cleaning and trimming are essential for breeds with long ears. Nail care is equally important, as overgrown nails can affect the dog's gait and overall appearance in the show ring.

Final Touches

Show dog grooming doesn't end with a well-maintained coat. There are additional finishing touches that can help a dog stand out in the ring.

- **Perfume**: Lightly spritzing the dog with a pet-safe grooming spray can add a fresh scent, enhancing the overall presentation.
- **Polishing the Coat**: For dogs with long coats, a light coat polish can be applied to give the fur a healthy, shiny appearance. This can help the coat catch the light in the ring, emphasizing its smooth texture and cleanliness.
- **Final Check**: Before entering the ring, it's important to give the dog a final once-over. Check for any stray hairs, dirt, or issues that could detract from the dog's appearance. A quick brush and a few final adjustments can ensure the dog looks its best when it steps into the show ring.

Show dog grooming is a specialized, time-consuming process that requires skill, patience, and an in-depth understanding of breed standards. From brushing and bathing to trimming, shaping, and special grooming techniques, each step is aimed at presenting the dog in its ideal form.

Chapter 6: DIY Grooming at Home

Grooming your dog at home is an excellent way to maintain their health, appearance, and overall well-being while strengthening the bond between you and your pet. While professional grooming is important for some breeds, many dog owners find that regular grooming at home is not only cost-effective but also a rewarding experience.

With the right tools, techniques, and knowledge, you can keep your dog looking and feeling their best in the comfort of your own home.

DIY dog grooming allows you to monitor your dog's health more closely, checking for skin issues, irritations, or injuries that might otherwise go unnoticed between professional visits.

It also helps build trust and can make the grooming process less stressful for both you and your dog, especially if done gradually and with positive reinforcement.

This chapter will guide you through the basics of home grooming, from brushing and bathing to nail trimming and ear care. It will highlight the essential tools you'll need and provide step-by-step instructions to ensure a safe and effective grooming session.

Whether you're grooming a puppy or an older dog, mastering these techniques will give you the confidence to handle your dog's grooming needs at home.

Setting Up Your Grooming Space

Creating the right environment for grooming your dog at home is essential for both the safety of your pet and your own comfort. A well-organized, safe, and calm grooming space can make the entire process much easier, more efficient, and enjoyable. Whether you're a first-time dog owner or an experienced groomer, having a designated grooming area will ensure that your dog's grooming sessions are smooth and stress-free.

Start by selecting a space that is quiet and away from distractions. Your dog will be more relaxed in an area where they feel secure, without loud noises or unfamiliar activities that may cause anxiety. Ideally, choose a space where you can easily clean up after the session, as grooming often involves shedding hair, water splashes, and pet dander. This space could be a designated bathroom, laundry room, or any room with enough space to move around comfortably.

The next key element is having the right equipment. You'll need a sturdy grooming table, especially for larger breeds, so your dog is at a safe height for grooming. A grooming table provides stability and control while keeping your dog in a comfortable position. If you don't have a table, a non-slip surface such as a towel or mat on the floor can work as well, though it may be less convenient for both you and your dog.

Consider the lighting in your grooming space. Adequate lighting will ensure that you can see all areas of your dog's coat and skin clearly. It also helps prevent accidents while trimming nails, working around sensitive areas, and checking for health concerns. A well-lit room with natural light or bright, adjustable lighting will make the grooming process safer and more efficient.

Next, organize all your tools in one place. Having easy access to your grooming tools will minimize distractions and make the process flow smoothly. Some essential tools you'll need include brushes, combs, clippers, scissors, nail trimmers, grooming wipes, towels, and shampoos. Invest in a storage solution such as a grooming cart, drawer system, or tool caddy to keep everything organized and within reach.

Additionally, a non-slip mat or towel is essential for your dog's comfort and safety. A mat with a textured surface will help prevent your dog from sliding around during grooming, while also ensuring that they remain steady and calm. For larger dogs, having a grooming helper or assistant may be necessary to keep your dog comfortable and in place.

To reduce the risk of injury, make sure that the grooming area is free of any sharp objects, heavy furniture, or anything else that could pose a threat to your dog. Keep all grooming tools in good condition, as dull blades or broken equipment can cause discomfort or accidents. Regularly inspect your tools for any damage to ensure that everything is safe for use.

Consider also your dog's comfort during the grooming session. Provide a comfortable place for them to rest during breaks if the session is lengthy. Depending on your dog's behavior, you might need to introduce the grooming space slowly, starting with short sessions to help them associate the area with positive experiences.

Finally, the environment should be calm and welcoming. It's crucial that your dog feels safe and relaxed throughout the grooming process. Using treats, positive reinforcement, and calming scents like lavender can help reduce anxiety and create a pleasant experience for your dog. Try to minimize distractions like loud noises or other pets in the area, as they can cause stress for your dog and interfere with the grooming process.

By carefully setting up a dedicated grooming space, you'll be prepared to handle your dog's grooming needs with confidence. Creating a comfortable, organized, and safe environment is key to a successful DIY grooming routine that benefits both you and your dog.

Step-by-Step Grooming Routines

Establishing a consistent grooming routine for your dog is crucial for their health and well-being. Regular grooming helps maintain a shiny coat, clean ears, healthy nails, and an overall sense of comfort for your pet. Whether you're new to dog grooming or a seasoned professional, knowing the best practices for each step of the grooming process can make a significant difference in how enjoyable the experience is for both you and your dog. Here, we will outline a detailed step-by-step grooming routine that covers all aspects of dog care.

Preparation and Gathering Tools

Before starting any grooming session, it's important to gather all the necessary tools. Having everything ready will make the grooming process smoother and prevent interruptions during the session.

Here's a list of essential grooming tools:

- **Brushes and Combs:** Choose the right type of brush based on your dog's coat type (e.g., slicker brush for mats, pin

brushes for long-haired dogs, bristle brushes for short-haired dogs).
- **Shampoo and Conditioner:** Look for products that are gentle on your dog's skin, especially if they have sensitivities or allergies.
- **Nail Clippers or Grinders:** A pair of sharp nail clippers or a nail grinder will ensure a safe and precise trim.
- **Ear Cleaner and Cotton Balls:** For cleaning the ears and preventing infections.
- **Grooming Table or Non-Slip Mat:** A stable surface is essential for keeping your dog secure and comfortable during the session.
- **Towels and Drying Tools:** For drying your dog after a bath, including microfiber towels and a blow dryer (set on low heat).

Step 1: Brushing the Coat

Brushing is the first step in any grooming routine. It helps remove loose hair, dirt, and tangles, which prevents mats from forming and reduces shedding. Depending on your dog's coat type, brushing may need to be done several times a week or even daily for longer-haired breeds.

1. **Start by choosing the right brush** for your dog's coat type. For example, use a slicker brush for a long-haired dog, a bristle brush for short-haired dogs, or a comb for dogs with curly or wiry coats.
2. **Begin at the head** and work your way down the body. Always brush in the direction of hair growth to prevent discomfort.

3. **Use gentle strokes** to avoid irritating your dog's skin. Be especially careful around sensitive areas, such as the ears and belly.
4. **Check for mats and tangles.** For dogs with longer or thicker coats, mats can form, so be sure to work through them with your fingers or a mat rake before using a brush.
5. **Brush the tail and legs.** These areas tend to collect tangles, especially for dogs with longer fur.
6. **Finish by brushing the undercoat**, if your dog has one. This is especially important for double-coated breeds to prevent mats near the skin.

Step 2: Bathing Your Dog

Bathing your dog is a crucial part of their grooming routine. Regular baths keep your dog clean, fresh, and free from parasites, dirt, and bacteria. However, it's important not to bathe your dog too frequently, as overbathing can strip the natural oils from their coat, causing dry skin and irritation.

1. **Prepare the bathing area** with warm water, ensuring the temperature is comfortable for your dog. Have all your bathing supplies within reach before starting.
2. **Wet your dog's coat thoroughly,** starting from the neck and working your way down the body. Avoid getting water into the ears, eyes, or nose.
3. **Apply the dog shampoo.** Choose a shampoo suited for your dog's skin type (hypoallergenic for sensitive skin, medicated for skin conditions, etc.). Lather gently, massaging it into the coat to create a rich foam.
4. **Rinse thoroughly.** Ensure that all shampoo is removed to avoid irritation.

5. **Condition your dog's coat.** If your dog has a longer or thicker coat, conditioning helps keep it soft and manageable. Apply the conditioner according to the instructions and rinse thoroughly.
6. **Dry your dog with a towel.** Pat your dog dry to remove excess water, paying special attention to the ears and paws.
7. **Use a blow dryer (optional).** For long-haired dogs, use a blow dryer on the lowest heat setting to speed up the drying process. Hold the dryer a few inches away from your dog to prevent burns or discomfort.

Step 3: Nail Trimming

Trimming your dog's nails is essential to prevent overgrowth, which can lead to discomfort or injury. Nails that are too long can get caught on furniture or the carpet and may even cause joint problems over time.

1. **Select the right nail clippers** (scissor-style or guillotine-style) or a nail grinder. Choose whichever tool you're most comfortable with.
2. **Hold your dog's paw securely,** and gently press the paw pads to extend the nails. Be sure to only trim the very tip of the nail.
3. **Identify the quick,** the pink area inside the nail. Avoid cutting this part, as it contains blood vessels and nerves. If your dog has dark nails, it can be difficult to see the quick, so trim in small increments.
4. **Trim one nail at a time.** If you're using a grinder, move slowly and carefully, allowing time for your dog to adjust to the noise and sensation.

5. **Praise your dog** throughout the process to keep them calm. If your dog gets anxious, take breaks between each paw or nail.

Step 4: Cleaning Ears and Eyes

Cleaning your dog's ears and eyes helps prevent infections and irritations. Regular ear cleaning can be especially important for breeds with floppy ears, as they are more prone to moisture buildup and ear infections.

1. **Check your dog's ears regularly** for redness, odor, or discharge. If you notice any unusual signs, consult your vet before cleaning.
2. **Use a dog-safe ear cleaner** and a cotton ball or pad to gently wipe the inside of the ear flap. Never insert anything into the ear canal.
3. **Wipe the outer corners of the eyes** with a soft, damp cloth or a special dog-safe eye wipe. If your dog has tear stains, using an eye wipe can help remove stains and keep the fur around the eyes clean.
4. **Avoid harsh chemicals.** Make sure to use products that are formulated specifically for dogs to prevent irritation.

Step 5: Grooming the Teeth

Dental hygiene is a crucial part of grooming, as poor dental health can lead to tooth decay, gum disease, and other health issues.

1. **Use a dog toothbrush and dog toothpaste** (never human toothpaste). Gently brush your dog's teeth, focusing on the gum line and back molars.

2. **Introduce tooth brushing slowly** if your dog is not used to it. Start with short sessions and gradually increase the duration.
3. **Incorporate dental chews** into your dog's routine to help with tartar buildup and keep their teeth healthy.

Step 6: Finishing Touches and Final Inspection

Once the grooming process is complete, it's time for a final check. Inspect your dog's coat for any missed tangles or mats. Brush any remaining areas and give your dog a final rubdown to help distribute the natural oils in their coat.

1. **Inspect for signs of irritation.** Check your dog's skin, ears, and paws for any signs of redness, irritation, or discomfort.
2. **Reward your dog with praise or a treat** after the session. This helps them associate grooming with positive experiences and can reduce anxiety for future sessions.
3. **Clean up your grooming space,** removing any hair, tools, or debris that may have accumulated during the session.

By following this step-by-step grooming routine, you ensure that your dog remains healthy, happy, and well-groomed. Regular grooming not only improves the appearance of your dog but also provides an opportunity for you to check for any potential health issues. Keep grooming sessions as stress-free as possible, and your dog will grow to enjoy the bonding experience.

Troubleshooting Common Grooming Challenges

Grooming your dog is an essential part of their overall care, but it is not always without its challenges. Every dog is unique, and certain grooming issues may arise based on factors like breed, temperament, coat type, or health condition. Understanding these challenges and how to troubleshoot them can help make the grooming process smoother for both you and your dog. By identifying and addressing problems before they escalate, you can ensure your dog remains healthy and happy while also keeping them well-groomed. This section will explore the most common grooming challenges and offer solutions for each one.

1. Fear and Anxiety During Grooming

Many dogs experience anxiety or fear during grooming sessions. This is especially common for puppies or dogs that have not been groomed regularly or have had negative experiences in the past. Fear and anxiety can make grooming more difficult and can even lead to behavioral issues.

Signs of Anxiety:

- Excessive drooling or panting
- Whining, barking, or growling
- Attempting to escape or hide
- Shaking or cowering

Troubleshooting Solutions:

1. **Start Slowly and Gently:** If your dog is fearful, begin grooming in small steps. Start by handling your dog gently,

and reward them with treats and praise when they remain calm. Gradually introduce grooming tools, allowing your dog to become accustomed to the sound, touch, and feel of each tool.
2. **Positive Reinforcement:** Use treats, praise, and even toys to reward good behavior during grooming sessions. This will help your dog associate grooming with positive experiences.
3. **Short Sessions:** If your dog is especially anxious, limit the grooming sessions to short, manageable periods. Over time, you can increase the length of the sessions as your dog becomes more comfortable.
4. **Desensitization Training:** For particularly nervous dogs, consider doing desensitization training by gently handling the areas of their body they dislike being touched. Over time, this will reduce fear and help them become accustomed to the grooming process.
5. **Calming Aids:** In cases of extreme anxiety, you might consider using calming products like pheromone sprays, anxiety wraps, or calming treats. These can help soothe your dog's nerves during grooming sessions.

2. Matting and Tangles

Matting is a common issue, especially for long-haired breeds. Mats occur when hair becomes tangled and forms tight clumps that can be uncomfortable for your dog. Matting is most common in areas like behind the ears, under the arms, around the collar, and along the legs.

Troubleshooting Solutions:

1. **Preventative Brushing:** Regular brushing is the best way to prevent mats and tangles. For dogs with long or thick coats, it is essential to brush them at least two to three times a week. Use a detangling spray or a mat comb to help loosen any knots before brushing.
2. **Work with Small Sections:** If you encounter mats, take your time working through them. Don't try to rip the mats out, as this can hurt your dog. Instead, gently work through the mats with your fingers, then use a slicker brush or comb to loosen the tangles. If the mats are stubborn, you may need to trim them out.
3. **Mats Around Sensitive Areas:** For areas like the ears and legs, where mats are more likely to form, use a comb or detangling brush designed for sensitive areas. Be gentle, as pulling or tugging can cause discomfort.
4. **Regular Grooming Appointments:** For dogs prone to severe matting, regular visits to a professional groomer may be necessary. Professional groomers have the experience and tools to remove mats without causing distress to your dog.

3. Nail Trimming Difficulties

Nail trimming can be challenging for both owners and dogs. Many dogs dislike having their paws handled, and trimming nails improperly can lead to injury or trauma. It's common for dogs to be nervous during nail trimming, and if done incorrectly, you may accidentally cut too close to the quick, causing bleeding.

Troubleshooting Solutions:

1. **Start Early:** If you have a puppy, introduce nail trimming at an early age. Gradually get your puppy accustomed to

having their paws handled and nails trimmed. This will make it much easier as they grow older.
2. **Use Proper Tools:** Invest in high-quality nail clippers or a nail grinder that suits your dog's size and nail type. Make sure the tools are sharp and in good condition to avoid any rough edges or splits in the nails.
3. **Take Small Trims:** Only trim small amounts at a time to avoid cutting into the quick. If you're unsure, trim just the tip of the nail to prevent injury. It's always better to trim little and often than to take off too much at once.
4. **Apply Styptic Powder:** If you accidentally cut into the quick and cause bleeding, use styptic powder to stop the bleeding. Keep a small container on hand for emergencies.
5. **Use Distractions:** If your dog is nervous, use treats or toys to distract them. You can also try trimming one or two nails at a time, offering praise and rewards between each one, to help your dog associate the process with something positive.

4. Skin Sensitivity and Irritation

Some dogs have sensitive skin that is prone to dryness, rashes, or irritation. Excessive grooming, harsh products, or allergies can all contribute to skin problems.

Troubleshooting Solutions:

1. **Use Hypoallergenic Products:** For dogs with sensitive skin, use grooming products that are hypoallergenic and free of harsh chemicals. Avoid shampoos with artificial fragrances or dyes, as these can irritate the skin.
2. **Moisturize Dry Skin:** If your dog has dry skin, consider using a dog-safe moisturizing balm or oil to help hydrate the

skin and coat. Coconut oil is a natural option that can be applied directly to dry patches of skin.
3. **Avoid Overbathing:** Frequent bathing can strip your dog's skin of natural oils, leading to dryness and irritation. Bathe your dog only when necessary, and always use a moisturizing dog shampoo.
4. **Consult a Veterinarian:** If your dog's skin problems persist or worsen, it's best to consult with a veterinarian. Skin conditions can be symptoms of underlying health issues like allergies, parasites, or infections that require medical attention.

5. Dealing with Excessive Shedding

Shedding is a natural process for dogs, but it can become problematic when excessive shedding occurs. While some breeds shed more than others, heavy shedding can cause a mess in your home and may be a sign of an underlying issue, such as poor diet, stress, or health conditions.

Troubleshooting Solutions:

1. **Brush Regularly:** Regular brushing is essential for managing shedding. Brushing helps remove loose fur and prevent it from collecting in your home. For dogs with heavy coats or double coats, invest in a de-shedding tool or an undercoat rake to help remove excess hair.
2. **Healthy Diet:** Make sure your dog's diet includes the necessary nutrients to maintain a healthy coat. Omega-3 and omega-6 fatty acids are particularly important for skin and coat health. If your dog's shedding seems excessive or unusual, consult your vet to rule out nutritional deficiencies.

3. **Hydration and Moisturization:** Dry skin can lead to increased shedding. Ensure that your dog is drinking enough water, and consider using moisturizing shampoos or sprays to maintain their skin's health.
4. **Consider Professional Grooming:** If shedding becomes unmanageable, professional groomers can help remove excess hair and give your dog a thorough bath to help control shedding.

6. Grooming a Dog with Special Needs

Dogs with special needs, whether due to medical conditions or physical disabilities, may require extra care during grooming sessions. These dogs may experience discomfort or difficulty with movement, making grooming a more complex process.

Troubleshooting Solutions:

1. **Consult with a Vet:** Before grooming a dog with special needs, consult your veterinarian to understand any specific precautions or needs related to their condition. For example, dogs with arthritis may have joint pain, requiring extra care during grooming.
2. **Gentle Touch:** When grooming senior dogs or dogs with physical disabilities, use a gentle touch. Be aware of sensitive areas and avoid putting pressure on sore spots or joints.
3. **Take Breaks:** If your dog becomes tired or stressed, take breaks during the grooming process. This will help your dog feel more relaxed and prevent exhaustion or discomfort.
4. **Adapt Tools:** Some grooming tools, such as nail clippers, may need to be adapted for dogs with special needs. Consult

a groomer or veterinarian to find tools that will make grooming more comfortable for your dog.

Grooming challenges are a normal part of the process, but with patience and the right approach, they can be effectively managed. Whether dealing with fear and anxiety, mats and tangles, or special grooming needs, understanding the issues your dog faces and implementing appropriate solutions is key to a successful grooming routine.

Chapter 7: Professional Grooming

While regular at-home grooming is essential for maintaining your dog's overall health and appearance, there are instances where professional grooming becomes necessary. Professional groomers possess the expertise, tools, and experience to handle tasks that may be challenging or too time-consuming for the average pet owner.

This chapter will explore the role of professional groomers, when to seek their services, and the benefits of professional grooming.

A professional groomer can provide a level of care that ensures your dog receives the best treatment possible, especially when it comes to breeds with complex grooming needs.

Whether your dog has a thick, long coat that requires detailed attention, or they're getting ready for a show, professional groomers are equipped with specialized skills to handle these tasks efficiently and safely.

Furthermore, professional groomers can spot early signs of skin conditions, infections, or other health issues during grooming sessions. This early detection can make a significant difference in your dog's health and well-being.

In this chapter, we'll discuss how to choose the right groomer, what to expect during professional grooming appointments, and how to prepare your dog for their visit, ensuring a smooth experience for both you and your furry companion.

When to Seek a Professional Groomer

While regular grooming at home can help keep your dog clean, healthy, and comfortable, there are certain circumstances where seeking the help of a professional groomer is not only beneficial but essential. Professional groomers are highly trained and equipped with the knowledge, skills, and tools needed to tackle more complex grooming tasks that might be overwhelming or difficult for you to perform on your own. This section will explore various situations where it's a good idea to take your dog to a professional groomer and the benefits of doing so.

Complex Coat Care Needs

Some dogs have coats that require specialized grooming techniques, which can be challenging for an inexperienced pet owner. Breeds like Poodles, Shih Tzus, and Schnauzers, which have curly, long, or thick coats, need regular trimming, clipping, and specific styling to prevent mats, tangles, and skin issues. Grooming these coats at home may be time-consuming, and without the proper tools, it can be difficult to achieve the desired results. Professional groomers have the expertise to properly manage these coats, ensuring they are not only aesthetically pleasing but also healthy and comfortable for your dog.

Handling Matting and Tangles

Matting and tangles are common in dogs with long, dense, or curly coats. While regular brushing can prevent mats from forming, there are times when mats become too tight or severe to handle at home. Matting can cause discomfort and even pain to your dog, especially if the mats are pulling at their skin or causing hot spots. In these cases, a professional groomer can safely and effectively remove mats without causing harm to the dog's skin. Professional groomers have the experience and tools to detangle mats without risking injury, such as using specialized combs or clippers designed for this task.

Breed-Specific Grooming Requirements

Certain breeds have grooming standards that are difficult to maintain without professional assistance. For example, show dogs must adhere to very specific grooming standards to meet competition requirements. Grooming for these dogs requires precision and skill that may be challenging for non-professionals. A professional groomer trained in show dog grooming can help your dog achieve the desired appearance, which is crucial for breed standard adherence and competition readiness.

Nail Care and Paw Pad Maintenance

Trimming a dog's nails can be a stressful task for both the dog and the owner. If not done correctly, nail trimming can lead to bleeding, pain, and anxiety for your dog. Professional groomers are experienced in safely trimming nails and can also tend to the sensitive paw pads. Additionally, they can provide expert advice on maintaining healthy paw pads, such as moisturizing cracked pads or preventing injuries from walking on rough surfaces. If your dog's nails are particularly thick, overgrown, or difficult to trim, it's a good idea to seek professional help to avoid causing injury.

Skin Issues and Health Concerns

A visit to a professional groomer is not just for beauty; it can also be a valuable opportunity for health checks. Groomers are trained to spot early signs of skin infections, parasites, or other health issues. They can notice issues like hot spots, rashes, lumps, or unusual skin conditions that may require veterinary attention. Some groomers even work closely with veterinarians, providing early detection of potential health problems before they worsen. If your dog is suffering from skin irritations, allergic reactions, or recurring conditions like flea infestations or dry skin, a professional groomer may be able to recommend treatments or direct you to a veterinarian for further care.

Senior Dogs or Dogs with Special Needs

Older dogs, or those with special needs, may require additional care and consideration when it comes to grooming. Mobility issues, arthritis, or sensitivity to touch can make grooming at home more difficult for both the dog and the owner. Professional groomers are skilled at working with senior dogs or those with physical limitations. They can take extra care in handling your dog gently and ensuring they are comfortable throughout the grooming process. Special tools or techniques, such as using a soft brush or offering extra breaks, may be employed to make the grooming session more pleasant for an elderly or ill dog.

High-Stress or Anxiety-Prone Dogs

Some dogs experience significant anxiety during grooming sessions, making it difficult for owners to carry out even basic grooming tasks at home. Dogs with high levels of fear or anxiety may not tolerate nail trimming, brushing, or bathing. In these cases, professional groomers are trained to work with anxious dogs and can provide a calm, patient, and soothing environment. Groomers may use techniques such as desensitization, positive reinforcement, and special grooming facilities to minimize stress and help your dog feel more comfortable. If your dog's anxiety makes grooming a challenge, a professional can ensure the process is as stress-free as possible.

Bathing and Coat Care for Dogs with Allergies or Sensitive Skin

Dogs with allergies or sensitive skin can benefit greatly from professional grooming. If your dog suffers from skin conditions such as dermatitis, hot spots, or eczema, you might struggle to find the right shampoos or techniques to avoid further irritation. Professional groomers have access to specialized products, such as hypoallergenic shampoos, soothing conditioners, and medicated treatments, to help alleviate skin issues. They can also use gentle grooming techniques to avoid aggravating sensitive skin and ensure your dog feels comfortable throughout the process.

Time Constraints and Lack of Proper Equipment

Some dog owners simply don't have the time or resources to keep up with regular grooming. Grooming can be time-consuming, especially for breeds with complex coat care needs. If you find yourself too busy to dedicate enough time to properly care for your dog's grooming needs, it's a good idea to seek the services of a professional groomer. In addition, some owners may not have the proper grooming equipment, such as high-quality clippers, brushes, or bathing tools, to effectively groom their dog at home. Professional groomers come equipped with the best tools and the expertise to use them efficiently.

When Grooming Becomes Overwhelming

There are times when grooming at home can simply become overwhelming, especially for first-time dog owners or those with multiple pets. If you're feeling unsure about how to properly groom your dog, or if the grooming process becomes too stressful, seeking a professional can take the burden off your shoulders. Professional groomers can also offer guidance on maintaining your dog's grooming routine at home, ensuring that you stay on top of their care between visits.

In conclusion, professional grooming is not just about aesthetics or pampering your pet; it's about ensuring your dog's overall health and well-being. Whether your dog requires specialized coat care, has medical conditions that need attention, or simply needs a break from the grooming process, a professional groomer can provide invaluable assistance. If you find yourself unsure of when to seek professional grooming, trust your instincts—if a task feels too difficult, risky, or overwhelming, it's always a good idea to call in an expert to ensure your dog receives the best care possible.

What to Expect During a Professional Grooming Session

When you take your dog to a professional groomer, it's important to know what to expect from the session so you can feel confident that your pet is in good hands. A professional grooming session involves several steps, and while it can vary based on the groomer, your dog's breed, and the services requested, there are common procedures that most grooming sessions will follow. Knowing these steps in advance will not only prepare you but also help ensure that your dog's grooming experience is as positive and stress-free as possible.

Below is an in-depth look at what typically happens during a professional grooming session.

Initial Consultation and Assessment

Before any grooming begins, most groomers will conduct a brief consultation with you to assess your dog's needs and your expectations. During this time, the groomer will ask about your dog's temperament, behavior, and any health concerns you may have. They will want to know about any past grooming experiences, allergies, or medical conditions that may impact the grooming process. This is also the time to mention any special requirements your dog may have, such as the need for a specific shampoo for sensitive skin or requests for a particular style or trim.

If your dog has never been groomed before or is particularly nervous, the groomer may ask about how they typically respond to grooming tasks like nail trimming or brushing. The groomer will use this information to tailor the session to your dog's needs, ensuring the best approach is taken. Depending on the grooming facility, they may also perform a quick evaluation of your dog's coat, skin, nails, and overall health before moving forward.

Bathing and Cleaning

Once the consultation is complete and your dog is ready for the grooming session, the first major step is usually the bath. Bathing serves several purposes: it cleans your dog's coat, removes dirt and debris, and prepares the coat for further grooming steps like brushing, trimming, or styling.

During the bath, your dog will be placed in a tub or bathing area specifically designed for pets. The groomer will carefully wet your dog's coat using lukewarm water and apply the appropriate shampoo. If your dog has sensitive skin, the groomer may use hypoallergenic or medicated shampoos. The shampoo will be worked through the coat to remove dirt, oils, and loose hair, followed by a thorough rinse. In some cases, a second wash may be necessary, especially if the coat is particularly dirty or if the groomer is preparing your dog for a style change.

After the bath, your dog may receive a conditioning treatment to help moisturize their skin and coat. This helps keep their coat shiny and healthy, especially if your dog's coat tends to be dry or brittle. If your dog has any skin issues, the groomer may apply specialized treatments to soothe irritation or heal minor conditions. Once the shampoo and conditioner are rinsed out, the groomer will dry your dog using towels and possibly a professional blow dryer designed for pets.

Brushing and Comb-Out

After your dog's bath, the next step is brushing and combing. This is a critical part of the grooming process, as it helps remove tangles, mats, and loose hair. For dogs with long, thick, or curly coats, brushing is often essential to prevent mats from forming, which can cause discomfort and skin issues. Professional groomers use high-quality brushes and combs to carefully work through the coat and detangle any knots.

During this process, the groomer will be able to spot any issues with your dog's coat, such as mats that need to be carefully cut out, dry spots, or areas where the hair may have been damaged. Brushing also helps stimulate blood circulation to your dog's skin and can contribute to overall coat health. If your dog has a dense or double-layered coat, the groomer may also perform an undercoat rake to remove excess undercoat hair, which helps reduce shedding and keeps your dog's coat healthy and clean.

If your dog has mats or tangles that cannot be brushed out easily, the groomer may need to use specialized tools like mat combs, de-matting tools, or even clippers to safely remove the tangled hair. The goal is to minimize discomfort for your dog and avoid damaging their skin.

Nail Trimming and Paw Care

A vital part of the grooming process is nail trimming. This is often one of the tasks that many pet owners struggle with, especially if their dog is fearful of having their paws handled. Professional groomers have the tools and experience to trim nails safely and effectively. They will carefully trim each nail to the appropriate length, taking care not to cut too close to the quick (the sensitive part of the nail).

If your dog has overgrown nails, the groomer may need to file or grind them down gently to avoid causing discomfort. For dogs that are particularly anxious about nail trimming, the groomer may use positive reinforcement, treats, or a calm, patient approach to help your dog relax.

Additionally, groomers will often check your dog's paw pads for debris, injury, or dryness. They may clean out any dirt or debris between the paw pads and apply paw balm or moisturizer to prevent cracking or dryness. If your dog has any foot-related issues, such as cracked pads or a tendency to develop calluses, the groomer can help address these concerns.

Ear Cleaning and Eye Care

Many professional groomers also perform ear cleaning and eye care as part of the session. This is important because ears can easily accumulate dirt, wax, and moisture, especially in breeds with floppy ears, leading to infections if not cleaned regularly. Groomers will use gentle ear cleaners to remove excess wax and debris, being careful not to cause discomfort.

For dogs with sensitive eyes, groomers can clean around the eye area to remove crusty discharge or tear stains. This is particularly important for breeds that are prone to eye issues, like Poodles, Shih Tzus, and Bulldogs.

If the groomer notices any signs of irritation, redness, or discharge during the ear or eye cleaning process, they will recommend that you consult a veterinarian for further evaluation.

Coat Clipping, Trimming, and Styling

Once your dog's coat has been properly cleaned and brushed, the next step is trimming, clipping, or styling. The extent of this process depends on the breed of your dog and the desired look. Some breeds, like Schnauzers or Cocker Spaniels, require regular trims to keep their coats neat and well-shaped.

If your dog is getting a full haircut, the groomer will use clippers, scissors, and shears to shape and style the coat according to your preferences. Professional groomers are skilled at achieving breed-specific cuts, which can range from simple trims to intricate styles that adhere to show dog standards. If you've requested a specific cut or style, such as a teddy bear trim or lion cut, the groomer will follow these guidelines.

If your dog is not due for a full cut but simply needs a little maintenance, the groomer will trim excess hair around the paws, face, ears, and tail to keep them neat and tidy.

Final Touches and Check-Out

Once all grooming tasks have been completed, the groomer will give your dog a final once-over to ensure that the coat is evenly trimmed, clean, and free from tangles or mats. They will also check the dog's ears, nails, and eyes one last time to make sure everything is in good condition.

After your dog is fully groomed, you will be able to pick them up from the grooming facility. The groomer will usually provide you with a summary of what was done during the session, any issues they observed, and any recommended follow-up care, such as regular brushing or nail trims. They may also offer tips on maintaining your dog's grooming routine at home until the next professional session.

In some cases, the groomer may give your dog a little treat or reward for being a good client during the session. Some grooming shops even offer packages that include additional services like a bow, cologne, or bandana to send your dog home looking and smelling extra special.

Professional grooming is an important part of maintaining your dog's health and well-being, and understanding what to expect during a session can help you feel more confident in the process. From the initial consultation and bath to the final touches and checkout, a professional groomer ensures that every aspect of your dog's grooming needs is addressed with care and precision.

Building a Relationship with Your Groomer

Building a strong, trusting relationship with your dog's groomer is essential to ensuring that your pet receives the best care possible. A professional groomer not only helps maintain your dog's appearance but also plays an important role in their overall health and well-being. By developing a good rapport with your groomer, you can ensure that your dog's grooming experience is positive and stress-free while addressing any specific needs your pet may have. Establishing this relationship is based on clear communication, trust, and mutual respect, which can lead to a lasting partnership between you, your dog, and the groomer.

Initial Meeting and Consultation

The first step in building a solid relationship with your groomer is through a thorough consultation at the start of your grooming journey. This is when you and the groomer can exchange important information about your dog's health, temperament, grooming needs, and any preferences or concerns. A professional groomer will take the time to listen to your specific needs and tailor the grooming session to your dog's unique requirements.

During this consultation, it's important to share any relevant details about your dog's behavior and any past grooming experiences, especially if your dog is nervous, has specific health issues, or requires special care. Clear communication at this stage helps set the groundwork for a successful grooming experience. The groomer will also assess your dog's coat, skin, and overall health and discuss grooming options with you based on their evaluation. Be honest about your expectations and ask any questions you may have about the process, the products used, or the groomer's techniques.

Trust and Consistency

As with any relationship, trust is vital in your connection with your dog's groomer. A trusted groomer will treat your dog with kindness and patience, paying close attention to your pet's comfort and emotional well-being throughout the grooming session. Building trust with the groomer takes time, especially if your dog is nervous or has had negative experiences with grooming in the past.

Consistency in grooming appointments is also key to building trust. By regularly bringing your dog to the same groomer, your dog will become more familiar with the environment and the groomer's techniques. Over time, your dog will begin to associate grooming sessions with positive experiences, making them less anxious or fearful. Consistent visits also allow the groomer to develop a better understanding of your dog's grooming needs, preferences, and any changes in behavior or health that may arise.

Open Communication

An open line of communication is essential to ensure that both you and the groomer are on the same page regarding your dog's grooming routine. After each grooming session, take the time to discuss how your dog did during the session. If the groomer noticed any changes in your dog's coat, skin, or behavior, they will usually provide feedback. Likewise, it's helpful for you to share your thoughts and observations, especially if there's something specific you'd like to address in the future.

If your dog has any grooming preferences or needs that you'd like the groomer to keep in mind, be sure to communicate them clearly. For instance, if you prefer a certain trim style or have concerns about using specific grooming products, make sure the groomer is aware. Good communication allows for adjustments to be made as needed, ensuring that each grooming session meets your dog's needs and your expectations.

It's also important to communicate with the groomer about your dog's behavior and temperament. If your dog tends to get anxious or nervous around grooming tools, let the groomer know. A good groomer will have the skills and patience to work with a nervous dog and will make adjustments to their approach to ensure your dog's comfort.

Understanding Grooming Limits and Preferences

Every dog is different, and part of building a strong relationship with your groomer is understanding and respecting your dog's individual grooming limits and preferences. Some dogs may have sensitive areas that require extra care, while others may be more tolerant of grooming tasks like nail trimming or ear cleaning.

By discussing your dog's grooming preferences and limits with your groomer, you can help them customize the grooming session to your dog's specific needs. For example, if your dog becomes stressed during nail trimming, the groomer may take extra time to desensitize your dog to the process, using positive reinforcement to make it a more pleasant experience. On the other hand, if your dog has a thick, matted coat, the groomer may need to use different tools or techniques to avoid discomfort.

If your dog has medical conditions that affect their grooming routine, such as arthritis or skin sensitivities, be sure to inform the groomer so they can make necessary accommodations. This could include using softer brushes, avoiding certain grooming methods, or adjusting the grooming schedule to prevent stress.

Mutual Respect for Each Other's Role

While your groomer's primary role is to care for your dog's grooming needs, you also play an important part in ensuring your dog is ready for their grooming session. Respecting the groomer's time, expertise, and approach can go a long way in strengthening your relationship. Being punctual for appointments, following the grooming guidelines provided by the groomer, and preparing your dog for the session (such as brushing out tangles before the visit) can help ensure that the session goes smoothly for both your dog and the groomer.

Likewise, respecting your dog's boundaries and being mindful of their temperament can help create a positive experience. If your dog shows signs of anxiety or stress during grooming, take note of what works best to calm them down and share this information with your groomer. A collaborative approach between you and the groomer creates a stronger bond, benefiting your dog's grooming sessions and overall well-being.

Continued Education and Feedback

As you build a relationship with your dog's groomer, it's important to continue learning about grooming techniques and maintaining open feedback throughout the process. Some groomers offer educational resources to help pet owners understand how to care for their dog's coat between grooming visits. This can include advice on brushing techniques, selecting the right grooming products, or handling common grooming challenges at home.

You can also ask your groomer for tips on maintaining your dog's health and grooming routine in between appointments. For example, they may recommend specific brushes, shampoos, or other grooming tools to use at home. Some groomers even offer follow-up services like deshedding treatments or coat care packages that can help extend the life of your dog's grooming session.

Additionally, don't hesitate to provide feedback to your groomer. If there's anything about the grooming session that you think could be improved, whether it's related to your dog's comfort, appearance, or care, let the groomer know. Positive feedback is equally important, as it helps the groomer understand what's working well and reinforces the bond you share.

Building Long-Term Trust

Trust is an ongoing process, and building a long-term relationship with your groomer takes time. By being patient and consistent, you can ensure that your dog's grooming experience remains a positive and stress-free part of their routine. When your dog trusts their groomer and feels safe in their care, grooming sessions can become a bonding experience rather than a source of anxiety or stress.

A strong, lasting relationship with your groomer benefits both you and your dog. It ensures that your dog receives the best grooming care, tailored to their individual needs, and fosters an atmosphere of mutual respect and understanding. As you continue to work together, your dog will become more comfortable with grooming sessions, and you will gain confidence in your groomer's abilities, leading to a healthier, happier, and well-groomed dog.

Building a positive relationship with your dog's groomer is a key component of your dog's grooming care routine. Through clear communication, trust, and a commitment to your dog's well-being, you can establish a partnership that benefits both your dog and you. By working together, you and your groomer will ensure that your dog always looks and feels their best, contributing to their overall health and happiness.

Chapter 8: Breed-Specific Grooming

Breed-specific grooming is an essential aspect of maintaining your dog's health and appearance. Each dog breed has unique characteristics that require tailored grooming techniques to ensure they remain comfortable, healthy, and looking their best. Understanding the grooming needs of your dog's breed is crucial for preventing issues such as matted fur, skin irritation, and discomfort. In this chapter, we will explore the specific grooming requirements for various dog breeds, focusing on coat care, maintenance, and the specialized tools and techniques needed for each one.

While some breeds have relatively low grooming needs, others, especially those with long or thick coats, may require regular care to keep their fur in top condition. Additionally, certain breeds have specific skin or coat conditions that necessitate extra attention or specialized products. Whether your dog has a short, sleek coat or a long, luxurious mane, breed-specific grooming ensures that you are addressing their individual needs.

Throughout this chapter, we will cover popular dog breeds and their unique grooming challenges, providing tips and guidelines for caring for them. Understanding these breed-specific needs will help you become more equipped to provide the best grooming care for your dog, keeping them healthy, comfortable, and looking their finest.

Popular Breeds and Their Unique Grooming Requirements

Every dog breed comes with its own set of grooming needs, influenced by their coat type, skin health, and genetic characteristics. Some breeds require frequent grooming to maintain their fur's health and appearance, while others are lower maintenance. However, every dog, regardless of breed, benefits from regular grooming to ensure their overall well-being. In this section, we will dive deep into the grooming needs of popular dog breeds, offering detailed insights into the specific grooming techniques, tools, and care required for each breed.

Labrador Retriever

Labrador Retrievers are one of the most popular breeds worldwide, known for their friendly nature and loyal companionship. Their short, dense, water-resistant coat is relatively low maintenance but still requires attention.

Grooming Needs:

- **Brushing:** Although Labradors have a short coat, they shed moderately year-round and experience heavier shedding during seasonal changes. Regular brushing with a medium-bristle brush or a de-shedding tool can help reduce shedding and keep their coat healthy.
- **Bathing:** Labradors tend to get dirty easily, especially if they love to swim or explore muddy areas. Bathe them every 4 to 6 weeks, using a mild, dog-specific shampoo to avoid drying out their skin.

- **Ear Care:** Labradors have floppy ears that can trap moisture, leading to ear infections. Regular ear cleaning is essential. Use a vet-approved ear cleaner and cotton balls to wipe away dirt and debris.
- **Nail Trimming:** Regular trimming is needed for their nails to avoid overgrowth, as they are active and may wear their nails down naturally, but not enough to prevent discomfort.

Poodle

Poodles are known for their curly, hypoallergenic coats, which require diligent grooming to prevent matting. They come in three sizes: Toy, Miniature, and Standard, all of which have similar grooming needs.

Grooming Needs:

- **Brushing:** Poodles need daily brushing to prevent mats and tangles in their dense, curly coat. Use a pin brush or a slicker brush to gently detangle their fur, paying special attention to the areas behind their ears, under their legs, and around their neck.
- **Bathing:** Regular baths are necessary to maintain their coat's softness and cleanliness. Bathing should be done every 4 to 6 weeks, using a gentle dog shampoo that helps maintain the natural oils in their coat.
- **Clipping:** Poodles require frequent trimming to keep their coats neat and manageable. A professional groomer can provide a "puppy cut" or other styles suited to your preference. Poodles also benefit from regular haircuts to prevent their coat from becoming overwhelming and to ensure they remain comfortable.

- **Ear Care:** Their floppy ears are prone to moisture buildup, so regular ear cleaning is crucial to prevent infections.

Shih Tzu

Shih Tzus are small, affectionate dogs with long, flowing coats that require regular grooming to prevent tangling and matting.

Grooming Needs:

- **Brushing:** Shih Tzus have a long, double coat that needs daily brushing. A comb with wide teeth is ideal for working through tangles, while a slicker brush can be used to smooth out the coat. Pay close attention to their underbelly, ears, and legs where mats tend to form.
- **Bathing:** Bathe your Shih Tzu every 3 to 4 weeks using a moisturizing shampoo to keep their skin and coat soft. Be sure to thoroughly dry their coat after each bath to avoid skin irritation.
- **Trimming:** Many Shih Tzu owners prefer to keep their dogs' coats trimmed short (a "puppy cut") to make grooming easier. Regular visits to a professional groomer are necessary to maintain the desired look.
- **Eye Care:** Shih Tzus are prone to eye discharge, so regular wiping of their eyes with a damp cloth can help prevent staining and irritation.

German Shepherd

German Shepherds are known for their intelligence, loyalty, and striking double coats. Their thick, dense fur requires regular maintenance to keep it clean, healthy, and free from mats.

Grooming Needs:

- **Brushing:** German Shepherds shed heavily, especially during shedding season. They have a double coat that needs brushing at least once a week to remove loose hair and prevent mats. During shedding season, daily brushing may be necessary to keep their coat healthy and to reduce shedding around the home.
- **Bathing:** Bathe your German Shepherd every 2 to 3 months or as needed if they get dirty or smelly. Be sure to use a high-quality dog shampoo that's gentle on their skin.
- **Ear Care:** Their large, upright ears can accumulate dirt and moisture, making regular ear cleaning important to prevent infections.
- **Nail Trimming:** Regular nail trimming is essential, as long nails can cause discomfort and difficulty walking.

Cocker Spaniel

Cocker Spaniels are known for their silky, medium-length coats that require regular grooming to maintain their beauty. Their ears, in particular, need special attention to prevent infections and matting.

Grooming Needs:

- **Brushing:** Cocker Spaniels have a long, silky coat that requires regular brushing to prevent tangling and mats. Brush their coat 3 to 4 times a week, using a pin brush or slicker brush to keep their coat tangle-free.
- **Bathing:** These dogs should be bathed every 4 to 6 weeks to keep their coat in top condition. Use a gentle dog shampoo and be sure to rinse thoroughly.

- **Ear Care:** Their floppy ears require regular cleaning to prevent buildup of wax, dirt, and moisture. Use a mild ear cleaning solution to wipe down the inside of their ears and help prevent ear infections.
- **Trimming:** Cocker Spaniels benefit from professional grooming every 6 to 8 weeks to trim their coat and maintain their breed-standard appearance.

Yorkshire Terrier

Yorkshire Terriers are small dogs with long, silky coats that require diligent care to maintain their stunning appearance. They are prone to tangling and matting if not groomed regularly.

Grooming Needs:

- **Brushing:** Due to their long hair, Yorkshire Terriers need daily brushing to avoid tangles and mats. Use a fine-toothed comb or a slicker brush to gently work through their coat.
- **Bathing:** Bathe your Yorkie every 3 to 4 weeks, using a mild, moisturizing shampoo to keep their coat shiny and soft.
- **Trimming:** Regular trimming is necessary to maintain their coat's appearance. Yorkies are often groomed with a short, manageable style to reduce the need for constant maintenance.
- **Ear Care:** While they have upright ears, their ears still require regular cleaning to remove any debris that may collect inside, especially if the dog spends time outdoors.

Border Collie

Border Collies are energetic, intelligent dogs that have a medium-length double coat that requires consistent grooming to maintain its condition.

Grooming Needs:

- **Brushing:** Border Collies have a thick double coat that sheds year-round, with heavier shedding in the spring and fall. Regular brushing 2 to 3 times a week helps manage shedding and prevents mats. During shedding season, more frequent brushing may be necessary.
- **Bathing:** Bathe your Border Collie every 2 to 3 months, or more often if they get particularly dirty from outdoor activities.
- **Ear Care:** These dogs have semi-erect ears, so regular ear inspections and cleaning are essential to prevent ear infections.
- **Nail Trimming:** As active dogs, their nails may wear naturally, but they should still be checked and trimmed regularly.

Bichon Frise

Bichon Frises are small dogs with a curly, hypoallergenic coat that requires regular grooming to prevent matting and keep their skin healthy.

Grooming Needs:

- **Brushing:** Bichon Frises need daily brushing to maintain their fluffy, curly coat. Use a slicker brush or a comb to keep their coat free from tangles and mats. Pay extra attention to

- areas like the armpits, underbelly, and behind the ears where mats tend to form.
- **Bathing:** They should be bathed every 4 to 6 weeks using a gentle, moisturizing dog shampoo.
- **Trimming:** Bichons require regular grooming and trimming to maintain their signature look. Many owners prefer a professional groomer to maintain their coat's structure and style.
- **Ear Care:** Due to their floppy ears, ear care is essential. Regular ear cleaning helps prevent infections.

Dachshund

Dachshunds come in three coat types: smooth, longhaired, and wirehaired, each requiring different grooming routines.

Grooming Needs:

- **Smooth Coat:** Dachshunds with smooth coats require minimal grooming, needing only occasional brushing to remove loose hair. They should be bathed every 3 to 4 months, or more often if they get dirty.
- **Longhaired Coat:** Longhaired Dachshunds require regular brushing to prevent tangles and mats. They should be bathed every 4 to 6 weeks, and their hair trimmed periodically to keep it manageable.
- **Wirehaired Coat:** Wirehaired Dachshunds need regular hand-stripping to maintain their rough texture and to prevent their coat from becoming too soft. Professional grooming is often recommended for this coat type.

Each dog breed has its own unique grooming requirements that reflect the characteristics of its coat and overall health. By understanding these breed-specific needs, you can provide the best grooming care for your dog, ensuring they are happy, healthy, and looking their best.

Tips for Mixed Breeds

When it comes to grooming, mixed breed dogs often pose unique challenges and opportunities. Since they inherit a combination of traits from their parent breeds, their grooming needs can vary widely depending on the coat types and characteristics they've inherited. However, understanding their grooming requirements is key to keeping them healthy, comfortable, and looking their best. Below, we explore how to manage the grooming of mixed-breed dogs, with a focus on common considerations, tips, and tricks.

Understanding the Coat Type of Your Mixed-Breed Dog

One of the most important aspects of grooming a mixed breed dog is understanding the type of coat they have. Since mixed breeds can inherit coat types from one or both parents, their coat care will depend largely on whether they have a short, long, curly, wiry, or double-layered coat. Here are the main coat types and their general grooming needs:

- **Short Coats:** Dogs with short coats, such as those from a Labrador Retriever or Beagle, tend to shed moderately. They require minimal grooming, but regular brushing can help reduce shedding and distribute natural oils throughout their coat.

- **Long Coats:** Mixed breeds with long coats, often inherited from breeds like the Shih Tzu or Yorkshire Terrier, will need frequent brushing to prevent tangling, matting, and overall hair buildup. Longhaired mixed breeds also require regular trimming and the occasional professional grooming session.
- **Curly Coats:** If your mixed breed has a curly coat, they may require a more specialized grooming routine. Curly-haired dogs, such as Poodles or Cockapoos, are prone to matting and tangling, so regular brushing and trimming are necessary to maintain a healthy, neat coat.
- **Wiry Coats:** Mixed breeds with wiry coats, like the Schnauzer or Fox Terrier, require regular hand-stripping to prevent their coat from becoming too soft. This type of coat is naturally protective and weather-resistant, but it can become matted if not cared for properly.
- **Double Coats:** Many mixed-breed dogs have double coats, meaning they have a dense undercoat beneath a topcoat. Breeds like Huskies, Golden Retrievers, and Border Collies are known for this coat type. Dogs with double coats need frequent brushing, especially during shedding season, to remove loose hair and avoid matting.

Creating a Regular Grooming Routine

Establishing a regular grooming routine for your mixed breed dog is essential for their health and comfort. Grooming doesn't just enhance your dog's appearance but also contributes to their overall well-being by preventing skin issues, mats, tangles, and even ear infections. Depending on the type of coat your dog has, your routine will differ.

- **Brushing:** Regardless of their coat type, most mixed-breed dogs benefit from brushing. Even short-coated dogs shed and will benefit from the occasional brushing to keep their coat smooth and remove excess hair. Long-haired dogs require more frequent brushing, ideally every day or every other day, to keep their coat in top condition. For curly or wiry coats, investing in specialized brushes such as a slicker brush or comb is important to prevent tangles and mats.
- **Bathing:** Bathe your mixed breed dog only when necessary, as excessive bathing can dry out their skin. The frequency of baths will depend on how much dirt or oil your dog accumulates, their activity level, and any potential skin issues. A general rule of thumb is to bathe your dog once every 4 to 6 weeks unless they have specific needs like a skin condition or a heavy-smelling coat that needs more frequent cleaning.
- **Nail Trimming:** Regular nail trimming is crucial for all dogs. Long nails can cause discomfort, and in severe cases, they can interfere with your dog's movement or cause injury. For most dogs, nail trimming should occur every 2 to 4 weeks, depending on how fast their nails grow and whether they are active enough to naturally wear them down.
- **Ear Cleaning:** Many mixed-breed dogs, especially those with floppy ears, are prone to ear infections. Regular ear checks and cleaning are vital, especially if your dog spends time in water or has a history of ear issues. Use a vet-approved ear cleaner and cotton balls to gently wipe the outer part of their ears. Avoid using Q-tips inside the ear canal unless instructed by a vet.
- **Teeth Brushing:** Mixed breed dogs, like all dogs, need regular dental care to prevent dental disease. Use dog-

friendly toothbrushes and toothpaste, and brush your dog's teeth 2 to 3 times a week to help reduce plaque and tartar buildup. Regular chewing on dental toys can also assist in maintaining dental hygiene.

Dealing with Shedding

Shedding is a common concern for owners of mixed-breed dogs. The amount and frequency of shedding will largely depend on the parent breeds. Some mixed breeds shed heavily, while others shed minimally.

- **Short-Haired Mixed Breeds:** Dogs with short coats tend to shed continuously throughout the year, though the amount may fluctuate with the seasons. Brushing them once a week or every other week can help reduce the amount of hair in your home and keep their coat healthy.
- **Long-Haired Mixed Breeds:** Long-haired dogs often shed less frequently but more heavily during certain times of the year. Regular brushing is essential to prevent mats and tangles, and using a de-shedding brush or rake can help manage the shedding during the peak shedding seasons (spring and fall).
- **Managing Shedding:** If you're concerned about shedding, consider using tools like de-shedding brushes, furminators, or grooming gloves to help remove excess hair from your dog's coat. You can also bathe your dog regularly (every 4-6 weeks) with a gentle dog shampoo that promotes shedding control, but be sure not to over-bathe them, as this can dry out their skin.

Common Grooming Issues for Mixed Breeds

With the combination of genes from various breeds, mixed-breed dogs can be more prone to certain grooming challenges. Understanding these potential issues can help you address them early and keep your dog's coat and skin in optimal condition.

- **Mats and Tangles:** Dogs with long or curly coats are prone to mats and tangles, particularly in areas like the ears, armpits, behind the legs, and under the belly. To prevent mats, make sure to brush your dog's coat regularly and work gently through any tangles with a wide-toothed comb or detangling spray. In some cases, you may need to cut out severe mats carefully to prevent skin irritation.
- **Dry or Itchy Skin:** Dry skin is common in mixed breeds with a variety of coat types, especially during the colder months or in dry climates. Regular bathing with a moisturizing shampoo and conditioning treatments can help relieve dryness. If the itching persists, it may be a sign of allergies or other skin issues, and you should consult your veterinarian for advice.
- **Overgrown Nails:** Mixed-breed dogs, especially those with active lifestyles, may naturally wear down their nails, but some dogs have trouble wearing them down enough, leading to overgrowth. Check your dog's nails regularly and trim them as needed to prevent discomfort and avoid injury.
- **Ear Infections:** Mixed-breed dogs with floppy ears, such as those with Cocker Spaniel or Basset Hound genes, may be more prone to ear infections. Always keep the ears dry, and clean them regularly with a vet-approved ear solution.

Dealing with Unique Grooming Needs

Some mixed breeds inherit specialized grooming needs depending on their lineage. For example:

- **Hypoallergenic Dogs:** Many mixed breeds inherit hypoallergenic traits from breeds like the Poodle or Bichon Frise. These dogs tend to shed less dander, making them a good choice for people with allergies. While hypoallergenic mixed breeds may not require as much shedding management, they do need regular grooming to keep their coats clean and mat-free.
- **Active Dogs with Short Coats:** If your mixed-breed dog is highly active, such as a mix with a sporting or working breed, they may develop skin conditions like hotspots or irritation from dirt, mud, or moisture. Ensure your dog's coat is thoroughly cleaned after outdoor activities, and use specialized shampoos for active dogs if needed.
- **Sensitive Skin:** Some mixed-breed dogs, especially those with thin or sensitive skin, may require special grooming products designed for their skin type. Using gentle, hypoallergenic shampoos and conditioners, as well as paying close attention to how your dog's skin reacts to different grooming routines, can help prevent irritation.

Grooming at Home vs. Professional Grooming

For many mixed-breed owners, grooming at home is an ongoing, rewarding task that deepens the bond between pet and owner. However, there are instances where professional grooming is necessary. For example, dogs with very thick, long, or curly coats may need a professional groomer to ensure they're trimmed correctly and to avoid skin injuries that could arise from improper trimming at home.

When to Seek Professional Grooming:

- When mats or tangles are too severe to remove on your own
- If your dog has a complex grooming pattern that you aren't sure how to manage
- When you need a specific breed cut or style
- If you're unsure how to trim areas like the ears, feet, or tail safely
- For professional nail trimming, especially for dogs that are afraid of nail clippers

Grooming a mixed-breed dog can be both a fun and rewarding experience, but it requires an understanding of their unique needs. By identifying your dog's coat type and adjusting your grooming routine to suit their specific characteristics, you can help keep your mixed breed healthy, happy, and looking their best.

Chapter 9: Advanced Topics in Grooming

Grooming is a multifaceted practice that goes far beyond basic brushing and bathing. While every dog requires a certain level of care, some dogs need more specialized grooming techniques due to their breed, health, or lifestyle. In this chapter, we will delve into advanced grooming topics that address the unique needs of dogs with special grooming requirements, as well as introduce advanced techniques that will help keep your dog's coat and skin in top condition.

Whether you're an experienced groomer or a dog owner looking to expand your knowledge, this chapter will explore various topics, including dealing with complex coat types, managing sensitive skin, and using professional-grade tools. Additionally, we will discuss advanced treatments for skin conditions, dematting techniques, and handling grooming challenges specific to aging dogs or those with health conditions.

By mastering these advanced grooming techniques, you can provide the highest level of care for your dog, ensuring that their grooming needs are met with precision and expertise. Understanding the deeper aspects of dog grooming will allow you to cater to your dog's individual needs, making grooming a more enjoyable and rewarding experience for both of you.

Creative Grooming: Hair Dyeing and Accessories

Grooming your dog can be an art form, and one aspect of dog grooming that has gained popularity in recent years is creative grooming, which involves styling your dog's coat in unique ways using hair dyeing, accessories, and other non-traditional techniques. While creative grooming can be fun and visually striking, it's essential to approach it with care, ensuring that your dog's safety and comfort come first. This section will explore how to safely and creatively enhance your dog's grooming experience using dyes and accessories, while also offering practical advice on how to balance style with your dog's health needs.

Hair Dyeing: A Colorful Approach

Hair dyeing for dogs has become a trendy way to express creativity through grooming, allowing pet owners to add vibrant colors to their dog's coat, creating bold and fun looks. However, it is essential to understand the risks and requirements that come with using dye on dogs. Unlike human hair dye, products designed specifically for pets are formulated to be non-toxic and safe for use on animals. These dyes are often made from natural, non-permanent ingredients such as vegetable-based dyes, which are less likely to irritate your dog's skin.

When choosing a dye, it is crucial to select a product that is explicitly labeled as safe for pets. You should also avoid dyeing sensitive areas, such as around the eyes, ears, and nose, where the dye could cause irritation or discomfort. Be sure to test the dye on a small patch of your dog's skin before applying it to the entire coat, to ensure that your dog doesn't have an allergic reaction.

Dyeing Techniques and Tips

Applying dye to your dog's coat requires precision and care. Here are some tips to help you achieve the best results:

- **Choose a Design:** You can create designs like stripes, spots, or ombre effects, or opt for an all-over color change. Start small with one section of the coat, such as the tail or a patch on the back, before expanding to more intricate designs.
- **Proper Application:** Always use gloves to protect your hands from the dye. Apply the dye using a brush or sponge and make sure to follow the instructions on the product. Keep the dye away from your dog's face and eyes.
- **Time It Right:** Leave the dye on for the recommended time, as instructed by the manufacturer, and then rinse thoroughly. It's important to use lukewarm water to avoid irritating your dog's skin.
- **Maintenance:** The vibrancy of pet-safe dye tends to fade after a few washes, so keep in mind that regular touch-ups may be required to maintain your dog's colorful look.

Safety First: Keeping Your Dog Comfortable

While hair dyeing can be a fun and unique way to express your pet's personality, safety is the top priority. Never use human hair dye on dogs, as it contains chemicals that can be harmful to them. Also, avoid using dyes that are not intended for use on animals, as these could lead to severe skin reactions. Some common signs of an adverse reaction include redness, swelling, or excessive scratching. If you notice any signs of discomfort after applying dye, immediately rinse your dog's coat with lukewarm water and consult a veterinarian if necessary.

Moreover, never force your dog into a grooming session if they seem stressed or uncomfortable. Creative grooming should be a fun bonding experience for both you and your pet, so if your dog isn't comfortable with dyeing, it's best to opt for less invasive ways to style them.

Creative Accessories: Adding Flair to Your Dog's Look

In addition to hair dyeing, there are numerous accessories you can use to enhance your dog's appearance. From simple bows and bandanas to more elaborate costumes and rhinestone collars, accessories can give your dog a fresh and stylish look without compromising their well-being. However, as with hair dyeing, it's crucial to choose accessories that are safe and comfortable for your dog to wear.

Here are some popular and safe accessories you can try:

- **Bandanas and Scarves:** These are classic accessories that can easily add style to your dog's look. Available in a variety of fabrics, patterns, and colors, they are simple to put on and remove. Bandanas can also serve a practical purpose, helping to keep your dog cool in the summer by absorbing sweat or excess moisture.
- **Rhinestone Collars and Leashes:** Adding some sparkle to your dog's collar or leash can be an elegant way to showcase their personality. However, be sure to choose rhinestone collars that are soft and padded on the inside, so they do not cause irritation. Additionally, opt for leashes that are sturdy and comfortable for walking.
- **Clothing and Costumes:** While not every dog enjoys wearing clothing, many small and medium-sized breeds

tolerate it well. There are numerous cute outfits available, from sweaters to costumes for holidays and special occasions. Be mindful of the fit; the clothing should not be too tight or restrictive.

- **Dog Hair Clips and Bows:** For dogs with longer coats, hair clips and bows are a great way to add some flair to their appearance. These accessories are easy to use and come in various shapes, colors, and sizes. Just ensure that the clips or bows are securely attached and not too tight, as this could cause discomfort.
- **Jewelry and Charms:** Pet jewelry, such as charm bracelets or necklaces, is another way to elevate your dog's style. Opt for lightweight, non-toxic materials that are easy to clean and won't cause chafing. When selecting a piece of jewelry for your dog, keep in mind that it should be designed specifically for pets and not for human wear.

Considerations When Using Creative Grooming Techniques

While creative grooming and accessorizing your dog can be a fun and enjoyable experience, it's important to always prioritize your dog's comfort and safety. Here are some key considerations to keep in mind:

- **Stress Levels:** Some dogs may not enjoy having their coat dyed or wearing accessories, so it's important to pay attention to their body language and behavior. If your dog seems stressed, try creative grooming on a less frequent basis and always focus on making it a positive experience.
- **Health Risks:** While pet-safe dyes and accessories are generally safe when used appropriately, it's essential to ensure that all products are non-toxic and safe for your dog.

- Avoid items with small parts that could be chewed or swallowed, as this could lead to choking hazards.
- **Professional Help:** If you are unsure about performing creative grooming techniques on your own, consider seeking help from a professional groomer. Many groomers now specialize in creative grooming and can offer expert advice and service. They can also recommend safe, high-quality products tailored to your dog's needs.

Creative grooming is an excellent way to add a personal touch to your dog's look, whether through colorful dye or stylish accessories. However, it's essential to approach these techniques with caution, using only safe and pet-friendly products.

Grooming as a Business: Starting a Career

Starting a career in dog grooming can be an exciting and rewarding venture. As more pet owners seek professional care for their pets, the demand for skilled groomers has grown significantly, making dog grooming a potentially lucrative business. Whether you're passionate about animals, looking to turn a hobby into a profession, or aiming to establish a full-fledged grooming salon, there are several key considerations and steps to take when starting a grooming business. This comprehensive guide will walk you through everything you need to know to start your own dog grooming career, from acquiring skills to setting up a professional space and marketing your services.

Understanding the Dog Grooming Industry

The pet grooming industry has seen a surge in popularity as more people view their pets as family members, willing to invest in their care and well-being. Dog grooming, in particular, has become a vital part of the pet care routine, with many breeds requiring regular grooming to maintain a healthy coat and prevent skin issues. In addition to traditional grooming services, specialized services such as creative grooming, mobile grooming, and even spa treatments have emerged, offering various niches to explore within the industry.

As a dog groomer, you can offer a variety of services, including washing, trimming, nail clipping, ear cleaning, and coat styling. Over time, you can expand your offerings to include other services such as flea and tick treatments, de-shedding treatments, and even pet styling for special events or shows. The beauty of the grooming industry is that you can tailor your business model based on your preferences, skills, and the demands of your target market.

Essential Skills and Training

While dog grooming may seem straightforward, it requires a combination of practical skills, knowledge, and experience to perform effectively and professionally. Understanding dog behavior, anatomy, and grooming techniques is crucial, as improper grooming can lead to injury or stress for the animal. For this reason, formal training is highly recommended, especially if you are new to the field.

Here are some steps you can take to acquire the necessary skills:

- **Enroll in a Grooming School:** One of the most effective ways to gain the skills needed for dog grooming is by attending a reputable grooming school. These schools typically offer certification programs that cover the basics of

grooming, dog behavior, and customer service. A well-established grooming school will teach you how to handle different coat types, use professional tools, and master essential grooming techniques.
- **Gain Hands-On Experience:** While formal training is helpful, real-world experience is essential in grooming. Many schools offer internship programs, where you can practice grooming on live animals under the supervision of experienced professionals. This allows you to develop your technique and become familiar with the practical aspects of grooming.
- **Stay Updated with Trends and Techniques:** The grooming industry is constantly evolving, and trends such as creative grooming, mobile grooming, and specialized dog spa treatments have become popular. Staying up-to-date on the latest grooming trends and techniques will allow you to offer fresh services to your clients and keep your business competitive.
- **Get Certified:** While certification is not always required to start a grooming business, obtaining certification from organizations such as the National Dog Groomers Association of America (NDGAA) or the International Professional Groomers (IPG) can boost your credibility. Being certified shows clients that you have met industry standards and are committed to providing quality care.

Creating a Business Plan

A solid business plan is essential for any startup, and a dog grooming business is no exception. Your business plan should outline your goals, the structure of your business, and how you intend to achieve success. A comprehensive business plan will also help you secure funding, manage expenses, and create a roadmap for growth.

Some key elements to include in your business plan are:

- **Business Structure:** Decide whether you want to run a mobile grooming service, set up a brick-and-mortar grooming salon, or start with a combination of both. Each structure has its advantages and challenges. Mobile grooming, for instance, can attract customers looking for convenience, while a salon-based business might offer a wider range of services.
- **Target Market:** Identify your target audience, which may include pet owners in a specific geographical area or clients with particular breeds or grooming needs. Understanding your target market will help you customize your services and marketing strategies to meet their demands.
- **Services Offered:** Outline the services you plan to offer. This could range from basic grooming (bathing, trimming, nail cutting) to specialized services (creative grooming, show grooming, or de-shedding). You can start small and expand your services as you grow.
- **Pricing Strategy:** Research the market to determine competitive pricing for your services. Consider factors such as the local economy, your level of experience, and the complexity of the services you offer. Be mindful that underpricing can devalue your services, while overpricing may drive potential customers away.
- **Marketing Plan:** A well-thought-out marketing strategy is essential for attracting customers to your grooming business. Consider both online and offline marketing techniques such as social media advertising, word-of-mouth referrals,

promotions, and loyalty programs. You can also partner with local pet stores, veterinarians, and animal shelters to increase your exposure.

Setting Up Your Grooming Space

Once you have completed the necessary training and created a business plan, it's time to set up your grooming space. Whether you opt for a mobile grooming unit or a stationary salon, your grooming environment should be clean, safe, and welcoming to both clients and their pets.

- **Location:** If you're opening a grooming salon, select a location that is easily accessible, preferably in a high-traffic area with a lot of foot or vehicle traffic. If you're operating a mobile grooming business, consider the areas you want to serve and ensure your vehicle is properly outfitted for grooming tasks.
- **Equipment and Tools:** Invest in quality grooming tools such as clippers, scissors, brushes, combs, and dryers. For mobile groomers, you will need a well-equipped van or trailer with the necessary plumbing, electrical setup, and safety measures. For a salon, ensure you have comfortable grooming tables, tubs, and dryers.
- **Hygiene and Safety:** Cleanliness is crucial in the grooming business. Your grooming space should be sanitized regularly to prevent the spread of parasites or infections. Additionally, safety measures such as non-slip mats, secure cages, and proper ventilation should be in place to ensure the comfort and safety of the dogs you groom.

Marketing Your Grooming Business

Effective marketing is key to the success of your dog grooming business. Building a loyal customer base requires continuous effort in promoting your services. Here are a few strategies to help you market your grooming business:

- **Create a Website and Social Media Presence:** In today's digital world, a professional website and social media pages are essential for attracting clients. Your website should showcase your services, pricing, contact information, and a gallery of before-and-after photos of your work. Social media platforms like Instagram and Facebook are perfect for posting grooming tips, photos of your work, and engaging with pet owners.
- **Referral Programs:** Word-of-mouth referrals are incredibly valuable in the grooming industry. Consider implementing a referral program that rewards existing clients for referring new clients. This can help you expand your customer base and build trust within the community.
- **Partner with Local Pet Businesses:** Partnering with local pet stores, veterinarians, and animal shelters can help promote your business. You can offer exclusive discounts or collaborate on events to increase your visibility.
- **Offer Seasonal Promotions:** Offering promotions around holidays, pet awareness months, or special occasions can draw in new clients and encourage repeat business.

Managing Your Finances

As with any business, proper financial management is crucial for your success. This includes setting a budget, tracking expenses, and managing cash flow. Some tips for managing your grooming business finances include:

- **Track Income and Expenses:** Keep detailed records of your income and expenses, including supplies, marketing, rent (if applicable), insurance, and employee salaries (if you have any). Use accounting software to simplify this process and stay on top of your finances.
- **Save for Business Growth:** Set aside funds for expanding your business, whether that means upgrading your equipment, hiring additional staff, or launching a larger marketing campaign.
- **Budget for Marketing and Advertising:** Allocate a portion of your earnings toward marketing and advertising, as this will help you attract new clients and grow your business over time.

Starting a dog grooming business can be a fulfilling and profitable career choice for animal lovers who enjoy working with dogs. By obtaining the right training, creating a solid business plan, setting up a safe and effective grooming space, and marketing your services, you can build a successful business that meets the needs of pet owners in your community. With dedication and passion, your grooming business can flourish and establish you as a trusted professional in the pet care industry.

Final Thoughts
Grooming as a Bonding Experience

Grooming is more than just a task to keep your dog looking good—it is an opportunity to build a deeper bond with your pet. Regular grooming sessions can help strengthen the relationship between you and your dog, allowing you to better understand their needs and behavior. Through grooming, your dog becomes accustomed to your touch and care, which helps foster a sense of trust and security.

When you spend time grooming your dog, you are engaging with them on a personal level, paying attention to their coat, skin, and overall well-being. This provides valuable moments for communication, as your dog will often respond to your actions with subtle signals of comfort or discomfort. By learning to read these cues, you can create a more positive grooming experience that reflects your understanding of their needs and sensitivities.

Additionally, grooming routines can promote a sense of relaxation and calmness for both you and your dog. Brushing, bathing, and other grooming activities can be soothing for your pet, particularly when done in a calm and gentle manner. This shared time together helps to establish a routine, making grooming a consistent part of your dog's life. It becomes more than just a necessary chore—it turns into a cherished ritual that strengthens the bond between you both.

The act of grooming also provides an excellent opportunity for early detection of health issues. By regularly checking your dog's coat and skin for signs of parasites, irritation, or changes in texture, you may be able to identify potential problems before they become more serious. This proactive approach not only ensures that your dog stays healthy but also builds a deeper connection as you take on the role of caregiver, attending to their needs and well-being.

Maintaining a Lifetime Grooming Routine

Grooming should be seen as an ongoing, lifelong commitment to your dog's health and happiness. Whether you have a puppy or an older dog, consistent grooming is essential for maintaining their physical health, emotional well-being, and overall quality of life. Establishing a grooming routine from an early age allows both you and your dog to become comfortable with the process, making it easier as they grow older.

The key to maintaining a successful lifetime grooming routine is consistency. Just as we follow daily hygiene routines to ensure our health, dogs need similar attention to their grooming needs. Regular grooming not only keeps your dog's coat looking great but also ensures that their skin remains healthy, nails stay trimmed, and ears are free from infection. Over time, your dog will learn to expect grooming as a natural part of their life, helping them remain calm and relaxed during the process.

A lifetime grooming routine also includes adjusting to the changing needs of your dog as they age. Puppies and young dogs often have more energy and less maintenance required when it comes to grooming. However, as dogs grow older, they may require more frequent care, particularly for their skin and joints. Older dogs may experience health issues such as arthritis or skin sensitivities, so the grooming process must be adapted to accommodate these changes. For example, using softer brushes, more frequent ear cleanings, or a gentler approach to nail trimming can help ensure that your senior dog is comfortable and happy throughout the grooming process.

It's also important to tailor your grooming routine to the specific needs of your dog's breed and coat type. Some breeds shed excessively, requiring more frequent brushing to prevent mats and tangles, while others may need regular professional grooming to maintain their coats. Understanding your dog's unique grooming requirements ensures that you can maintain their health and appearance without causing unnecessary stress.

Maintaining a lifetime grooming routine also involves caring for your dog's health and comfort beyond just their coat. Regularly checking your dog's paws for cuts, cracks, or debris, inspecting their ears for signs of infection, and ensuring their teeth are clean and healthy all contribute to their overall well-being. These practices ensure that you stay on top of your dog's needs, promoting a happier, healthier life for your furry companion.

As part of this routine, it is important to use the right products and tools. Using high-quality shampoos, conditioners, and grooming tools designed specifically for dogs can help maintain the health of their coat and skin. Avoid using human products on your dog, as their skin has a different pH balance. Additionally, keeping grooming tools clean and well-maintained ensures that they perform optimally and prevent the risk of injury to your dog.

Building a relationship with a professional groomer is also beneficial in the long term. A professional groomer can help you maintain your dog's grooming routine, especially for breeds that require specialized care. Establishing a relationship with a groomer who understands your dog's specific needs and preferences will help make grooming appointments smoother and more enjoyable for your dog. Moreover, a groomer can provide advice and tips that can assist you in maintaining your dog's grooming routine at home.

Another key aspect of maintaining a lifetime grooming routine is patience. Dogs are individuals with unique personalities, and some may not enjoy grooming as much as others. It's important to be patient, gentle, and consistent in your approach, gradually increasing the length of grooming sessions and allowing your dog to become accustomed to the process. Over time, grooming will become an enjoyable, routine activity rather than something to dread.

Grooming is a fundamental part of a dog's life, impacting not only their physical health but also their emotional connection with their owner. By seeing grooming as a bonding experience and making it a consistent part of your dog's life, you can ensure their happiness, comfort, and well-being for years to come. A well-maintained grooming routine enhances your dog's overall quality of life, providing both health benefits and a deeper connection between you and your beloved companion.

As you maintain a lifetime grooming routine, remember that grooming is not just about keeping your dog looking their best—it's about ensuring they feel their best too. Whether you handle grooming at home or seek the help of a professional, your commitment to your dog's grooming needs will enhance their overall health and strengthen your lifelong bond. Your dog's grooming journey should evolve with them, ensuring that no matter their age or health condition, they receive the care, love, and attention they deserve.

Farewell Message

As we reach the end of this journey through the world of dog grooming, I want to take a moment to reflect on the incredible connection that has been built between us and our beloved canine companions through every brush stroke, every grooming session, and every moment shared in the pursuit of health and happiness. Grooming is more than a simple task—it's an act of love, a means of deepening the bond between you and your dog, and an essential part of caring for your furry friend in a way that enhances their life in profound ways.

Throughout this book, we've explored the importance of grooming from a holistic perspective, offering you the tools, knowledge, and insights to care for your dog in the most thoughtful and effective way possible. Whether you've just begun your grooming journey or are a seasoned pro, the essence of dog grooming is always about compassion, patience, and a deep respect for the animal by your side. As you continue your grooming adventures, always remember that each moment spent with your dog is a moment of connection and care. These grooming routines aren't just about maintaining appearances—they are about ensuring your dog's health, comfort, and well-being, fostering trust, and creating a lifelong partnership filled with love and joy.

I want to encourage you to take what you've learned here and apply it to every aspect of your dog's life. Grooming is a ritual that should be enjoyed, a shared time for both of you to connect, and a beautiful way to ensure your dog lives their happiest, healthiest life. Never underestimate the power of your hands, the love behind every grooming session, or the impact it has on your dog's happiness.

Remember that the time and effort you dedicate to your dog's grooming needs—whether it's brushing, bathing, trimming, or simply spending quiet moments together—are some of the most valuable you can invest in your dog's overall well-being. Don't let it become a chore, but rather a cherished ritual that will keep your dog looking and feeling their best for years to come.

As you move forward with the tools, knowledge, and techniques shared in this book, I encourage you to take pride in your grooming journey. The more you invest in your dog's grooming, the more they will trust you, love you, and flourish under your care. Their coat will shine with health, their paws will remain strong, and their spirit will soar because of the love you've given them in these grooming moments.

I believe in you as a dog owner and as a caretaker of your dog's health, beauty, and happiness. You are equipped now with everything you need to continue this beautiful journey of dog grooming—one that will bring endless rewards of trust, companionship, and joy. Grooming isn't just about appearance; it's about ensuring a lifetime of health, comfort, and love.

Thank you for taking this journey with me. I hope this book has inspired, educated, and empowered you to approach dog grooming with a passion and devotion that will carry on for years to come. May you and your dog share many more moments of peace and connection in the future, grooming side by side. The bond you have with your dog is one of the most special gifts in the world—cherish it, and may every grooming session serve to strengthen it even more.

With all my heart, I wish you and your dog the best as you embark on the lifelong adventure of care, love, and companionship. Your dog's happiness, health, and well-being are in your hands—and I have no doubt that you will continue to be the best caregiver, companion, and grooming expert your dog could ever have. Keep grooming, keep loving, and keep cherishing every moment with your dog. This is just the beginning of an extraordinary journey.

WISHING YOU ALL THE BEST
DR. RUBY LUCAS
27TH DEC. 2024